The Short

Sweet Dream

of Eduardo

Gutiérrez

ALSO BY JIMMY BRESLIN

JIMMY

BRESLIN

THREE RIVERS PRESS
NEW YORK

The Short

Sweet Dream

of Eduardo

Gutiérrez

Published by Three Rivers Press, New York, New York.
Member of the Crown Publishing Group, a division of Random House, Inc.

www.randomhouse.com

THREE RIVERS PRESS and the Tugboat design are registered trademarks
of Random House, Inc.

Originally published in hardcover by Crown Publishers,
a division of Random House, Inc., in 2002.

Printed in the United States of America

Design by Leonard Henderson

Library of Congress Cataloging-in-Publication Data
Breslin, Jimmy.
The short sweet dream of Eduardo Gutiérrez / Jimmy Breslin.
1. Gutiérrez, Eduardo, 1978–1999.   2. Alien labor, Mexican—
New York—New York—Biography.   3. Illegal aliens—New York—
New York—Biography.   I. Title.
HD8085.N53 B74 2002
331.6'272'07471092—dc21   2001047283

ISBN 1-4000-4682-3

First Paperback Edition

For

TERESA GUTIÉRREZ DANIEL

For

AWILDA CORDERO

For

MAURICE PINZON

CHAPTER ONE

Tomás Eduardo Daniel Gutiérrez was the first-born of a fifteen-year-old mother in the town of San Matías Cuatchatyotla in central Mexico, about three hours by car from Mexico City. Daniel is his father's last name and Gutiérrez is the mother's. The baby was familiarly called Eduardo Daniel, but the official records used the formal name, Tomás Eduardo Daniel Gutiérrez. A midwife assisted. He was born on a Sunday morning, which allowed his father to be present. The father was away on the other six days, traveling by truck to sell loads of bricks. Sometimes he was given the wrong address for the customer, and he wound up driving for an entire day around Mexico City, selling the undelivered bricks door to door.

San Matías Cuatchatyotla starts as an alley running from the two-lane highway going to Puebla in central Mexico, forty-five minutes away. The alley is a Third World dirt path that runs straight through the dust with children leaning against walls and young mothers standing aimlessly on street corners holding staring babies, and dogs coated with flies sleeping in the alleys or walking in circles

1

in front of entranceways to shacks. Old women walk bent in the
heat and the flies. Their legs are thick and the grandchildren's thin,
but this does not matter. All in San Matías, body bowed or lithe,
have legs that can walk a thousand miles.

The alley runs into a network of other dusty alleys. They are
lined with one-story sheds and lots filled with bricks. At first, the
brick piles seem to be unfinished buildings, but then a kiln shows its
hot sides to display the town's business, baking bricks.

Papers by archaeologists say that fired bricks used in the construction of a temple in the area disputes the conventional belief
that only the Mayans built structures in this region. Fired bricks
were not Mayan; they were from the Roman Empire. All these centuries later, archaeologists say the bricks of San Matías are relics not
of the Mayans but of people from Europe—you figure out how
they reached here. The physical evidence says they did.

The official address of Eduardo's birth was number 8 Calle
Libre, that figure scratched on the wall at the start of the alley that
runs to a green tin fence with a door in it. A loud knock, and the
door is opened by a child with a dog leaning against its legs. The
hour of day, day of week, or time of year doesn't matter, for there is
always a child with a dog at the door. The doorway opens to a
crowded yard that has a large evergreen tree and is lined with concrete huts of single-room size that have flat roofs and curtains over
the doorways. The thirty members of the Gutiérrez family (the next
baby makes thirty-one)—uncles, cousins, nephews, nieces, dogs—
brush through the curtains. There are no toilets or showers. Water
is pulled up from the deep old stone well in a heavy wooden
bucket with great effort by women whose mouths contort and
whose bare arms throb as their large hands go one over the other
in pulling up the bucket. On a long table there is a row of seven
plastic buckets for washing dishes and pots and scrubbing clothes.
Dogs lap up soapy water in spill buckets on the ground. The
women hang wash on lines tied to the evergreen tree. The clothes

flap just above rabbits in wood cages. There are chickens in a wire pen, and dogs covered with flies spread out on the ground, peaceful now but not always.

On the day Eduardo was born, the father, Daniel, waited in the courtyard while the women washed dishes and clothes.

"Somebody always washes," he recalls. "When somebody dies, they wash. When somebody is born, they wash."

Eduardo's mother, Teresa, was shy to the point of agony. She spoke to nobody but her family. She left the house only when she heard the church bells up the street ring three times for the start of mass, or to buy something she needed. Each time, she draped a blue scarf over her face, Middle Eastern style. Everybody knew the scarf, but no one knew her, although San Matías is a small place. Eduardo was born with the deep shyness of his mother, but what directed body and life was neither home nor nationality. Mexico is just the name of a country, which comes from Mexica, another name for the Aztecs.

Eduardo's life came from the lines circling a globe.

Latitude rules.

CHAPTER TWO

Eduardo was born in a room off this courtyard with the sky above determining from the instant of his birth who he was and would be and how he would live the rest of his life. He cried into the world on June 15, 1978, at 19 degrees, 3 minutes north of the equator, and 4 degrees below the tropic of Cancer, in a place where the sun strikes the earth and those on it nearly directly. The path of the sun in the sky over San Matías is virtually the same each day of each year. Months are words. Seasonal changes carry the weight of a falling leaf. Each morning the sun rises straight up in the sky, to 80 degrees. For six hours each day in San Matías, for all the days, the burning eye of the sun stares unblinking and straight down. There are no shadows in its remorseless glare. The people at this latitude all have brown skin, often running to black. They must have it or they die in the sun.

All over the earth, the sun strikes from different angles. In Norway the sun gets half as high as over Mexico, 40 degrees, and comes at the earth on the oblique. People can't cast a shadow to equal their height. The sun must be 45 degrees before that can be done. In New York, except for June 21 and the days around it, the sun makes high sweeps across the sky, and the direct burning it does lessens by the day until December.

In the latitudes between 23½ degrees north, the tropic of Cancer, and 23½ degrees south, the tropic of Capricorn, the earth steams eternally, and most inside those lines are born with hues that often cause the whites above the tropic latitudes in the north to be somewhat apprehensive. Mexicans don't cause white foot races so often as the blacks; many Mexicans have slightly lighter skin, which makes them a little less frightening. Therefore businessmen and housewives see the Mexicans as the most worthy of all workers: The Mexicans are cheap labor.

Their heritage is Mexican by map and tongue, but latitude rules their bodies. The largest organ of the body is the skin, 6 percent of the body weight, whose hue originated so many millions of years ago. Color is spread through the skin by pigment that comes in drops so small that they fall beneath our ability to weigh them. Yet you put them together, the skin and the weightless pigment, and they can move the earth more than an earthquake.

In skin of any hue, the major cell population is the basal keratinocytes. There is a lesser group known as the melanocytes, whose effect is eternal. The number of melanocytes is the same in all skin: one melanocyte for every four to ten keratinocytes. Melanocytes contain granules called melanosomes, which carry melanin, the pigment that colors the skin. They bring pheomelanin, a light yellow or auburn, or eumelanin, which is dark brown.

In those latitudes near the equator, the sun blazing straight down for all those millennia has caused the melanocytes to be very active, producing large amounts of eumelanin. As in people of any color, the melanin granules rise to cover the keratinocytes' nuclei, protecting them from the effects of ultraviolet radiation. In so doing, the pigment colors the skin dark brown, or into shades of black. This skin color has nothing to do with intelligence, size, or athletic ability. It has to do with survival.

The dark pigment was first put into the body by nature—and beyond that the hand of God—to darken the skin and pass this hue down and thus protect all who follow against melanoma, a merciless killer. Melanoma starts with a genetic mutation of a cell caused by the ultraviolet rays of the sun. Ultraviolet rays bathe the white skin to death. It provides no defense. Black skin is a fortification. Melanoma, this abnormal growth of tissues, is uncontrolled, has no expected endpoint, and is furiously aggressive; it spreads like splashed acid. Then it kills from all the places of the body that it has touched.

People are born colors from tan to black in order to save them from being white.

Latino or Hispanic identity is as muddied as the waters of the Rio Grande. Color is of so many gradations that it confuses anybody with an official chart trying to count by race and hue. The combination of European and Indian heritage, with skin color thrown in, makes for a complex Hispanic concept of race.

The writer Richard Rodriguez noted, "I used to stare at the Indian in the mirror. The wide nostrils, the thick lips. Such a long face—such a long nose—sculpted by indifferent, blunt thumbs, and of such common clay. My face could not portray the ambition I brought to it. What could the United States say to me? I remember reading the ponderous conclusions of the Kerner Report in the sixties: two Americas, one white, one black, the prophecy of an eclipse too simple to account for the complexity of my face. Mestizo in Mexican Spanish means mixed, confused. Clotted with Indian, thinned by Spanish spume."

At each election, when New York added up ethnic voting, the total of non–Puerto Rican Hispanics was minute and the Chinese were listed as "other." There was only black and white.

Into New York they came, these people of every shade, from African black to Mexican and Indian brown and Chinese yellowish tan, people with dark eyes and straight black hair. They changed the city forever, including strong, proud white Queens, the place of cops and firemen, of the late Carroll O'Connor, who came from under the Jamaica Avenue el to become Archie Bunker. Suddenly the sidewalks were crowded with continents of children running through the gates of schools like P.S. 69 at the end of the day. Then one afternoon, a woman named Quinn who lived in Rosedale, outside Kennedy Airport, complained about the schools and as proof of her lack of prejudice said, "And I'll have you know that my son goes to a school that is ninety-nine percent minority. That's right. He goes with ninety-nine percent minorities." This school has pupils from seventy countries who speak forty languages. On this afternoon, the day before St. Patrick's Day, the kids had on green cardboard hats that they had made in class. Here came a little girl from India, with her Irish green hat tilted over dark hair.

"What's the green for?" she was asked.

"St. Patrick."

"What does he mean?"

"A parade."

"What kind of parade?"

"White people."

She had just identified the New Minority in New York.

As the 2000 census showed, there are now two types of people in the city. There are those of color. And there are those without color. Those of color are a large majority.

The old minority of the city is now the majority. The old majority is now the minority.

CHAPTER THREE

At age four, Eduardo Gutiérrez walked behind his father through the tin gate, out of the alley, and a few yards up to the brickyard. They passed a pit where a small pack of shrieking dogs leaped and clawed the dirt sides, teeth bared, trying to climb straight up and race through the streets and tear somebody to pieces. Each day when the sun rose to the top of the sky, instead of dozing while their fleas leaped, the dogs went heat crazy. Eduardo's father, Daniel, took the dogs from his yard and the alley and any strays and threw them into the pit, where they screamed for revenge until their mouths cooled in the evening shadows and he lifted them out.

Spread out on the dirt brickyard were long rows of gray cement slates used for roofing, called *tabiques* but considered bricks. There were also stacks of regular bricks awaiting a truck. The slates were drying in the sun. There were hundreds of them, arranged like cards in solitaire. Right away, Eduardo's uncle Tomás, sixteen, went up to the lines of slates and grabbed the last one in line, with the top of it under the bottom of the next slate, causing all the slates to slip down, one atop another. Tomás made a stack of ten slates in his hands. He carried them to the shed, where Eduardo's father placed them in stacks for more airing before they would be sold.

Eduardo's twelve-year-old nephew Jaime took four of the slates and, pressing them against his stomach, carried them to the shed.

Behind the older boys, his bare feet causing the dust to rise, came Eduardo with a single slate in his hands, all he could lift.

"You see," the father called out, "this is how you learn. My son is little. He learns so much in bricks."

Three years later, when Eduardo could carry four slates, his father said he had a skill with the slates and bricks that would be with him for the rest of his life.

"Yes, school is very important," the father said. "It is also important that he learns a skill so when he leaves school after the sixth year he can work and help his family."

When he was old enough to carry four slates, Eduardo was asked: "Which do you like, school or work?"

"*Trabajo!*" Eduardo called out.

The school was the one-story Benito Juárez School, a few blocks up Calle Libre. Looking up the street from Eduardo Gutiérrez' alley at number 8, you can see low posts placed permanently to block trucks and horse carts from passing in front of Our Lady of Guadalupe, one of 365 Catholic churches in the Cholula area. There is a plaza and a walk on a path under trees to enter the yellow church with red trim, which has insides of gold. After the church, the street continues through the same dust and flies, and the same children in doorways and young women holding babies, until it narrows to the eyes under the hot sky.

A block up from the church, one large truck, here to haul bricks, raises a cloud of dust that obscures most of the street.

On one desolate street corner there is the school, where Eduardo sat at a scarred white wood desk. The learning was difficult because nearly all the kids in the school knew they would go only as far as the required sixth grade, after which, at age twelve, they would go out to work, as do 90 percent of Mexican grammar school pupils. There are charges for junior high school. Books must be bought. There is a 320-peso bill, about $30 American, for tuition, and then charges for administrative costs and building repairs needed during the school year. The taxes do not cover this because the tax money is openly stolen by politicians in Mexico City. The payments don't seem high, 30 pesos here, another 30 there, but families feel that not only is it intolerable that kids who should be doing some of the heavy lifting at home are wasting the day in a schoolroom, but it is not right that the family has to pay for this injustice. Having a kid come straight home for a big free dinner after school on a day when he didn't even try to lift something is the sacrifice that hardens the heart.

In Eduardo's fourth-grade class, all parents had to appear on the next-to-last day of school to collect report cards. Mostly mothers did this. While Eduardo's mother signed all his report cards at home, she was too shy to go to the school and pick it up. The father showed and was instantly angered when Eduardo's card said he had not been promoted.

The father went home and told Eduardo, whose mood immediately turned dark—but not nearly as much as that of the father, who told Eduardo that instead of finishing school in two years, now it would take him three more years. This meant that the father would have to wait an extra year before he had a son giving full-time help in the brickyard.

It was the start of a life for Eduardo Gutiérrez that was to allow him to see nothing in San Matías other than the dirt and dust and flies. He lived in the end room in the compound with an uncle, two brothers, and various cousins. When he heard older people in town talking about going to America, he thought of going there to get money so he could build a new room in the one space left in the dusty compound. He would build the one room and a second atop it. He saw an iron staircase going up to it. He would paint the outside blue.

Dreaming, he could look to the north, to a sky of many colors billowing with white clouds. Somewhere up there—he knew because everybody said so—was a place of excitement and money. Breathing the sultry air on Calle Libre, he could not smell the air of Brooklyn, of Middleton Street in Williamsburg, with buses and an el, and streets so often cold and wet, and of the sound of creaking building walls.

ALL HIS YOUNG DREAMS gave him no idea of the dangerous path ahead. The young dream of everything except death. There was no vision of working alongside Nelson Negrón, for example, who cannot read or write in Spanish or English and who does what he is told, climbing the scaffold until he is chest high to the third level of a construction site on Middleton Street in Williamsburg, in Brooklyn, his right side straining under the fifty-pound sack of cement on his shoulder, looking up at a roof that is being held aloft by virtually nothing. If there are no roof beams, he reasons, what could there be under this third floor he is about to throw his sack onto?

There are twenty workmen crawling over the row of three-story brick condominiums being built. If the builder were legit, the workers would cost him about $15,000 a week. But the builder is Eugene Ostreicher, a man in his middle sixties who fled Hungary in 1944. He hires mainly Mexicans, and they take short money and like it or they're gone and Ostreicher finds somebody else for the same or less. His Mexican payroll is $5,000 a week.

Negrón is looking up at Eduardo, who is standing on a deck that moves when something is dropped on it.

In San Matías, Eduardo could not see himself here on this deck.

"The boss told me he wants it this way," Eduardo says.

Negrón drops the bag from his shoulder and shoves it at Eduardo's feet.

The floor went up and down.

"It's going to go down," he told Eduardo.

ACROSS THE STREET from the Benito Juárez School was an open-air tortilla store. A young woman in black stood at the end of a moving belt, and as a tortilla came off, smoking hot, she grabbed it with her right hand and snapped her wrist as if pitching a baseball, making the tortilla flip over, taking some of the heat off her fingers. She put the tortilla on a stack and immediately, continuing the motion, grabbed the next hot one from the moving belt. Every few moments another young woman took the growing stack of tortillas over to a counter, draped a towel over them, and sold them to people coming down the street.

The two jobs do not change, ever. Neither does the pay. Twenty dollars for a seventy-hour week.

Next to the tortilla store was the tiny box of a store where Silvia Tecpoyotti's mother, Olivia, watched the group of teenagers growing into men, one of whom could be for her daughters. Olivia Tecpoyotti Daniel sat in her store on the dirt street, a crammed closet of a store. She sold socks, packs of crayons and boxes of white paste for children's projects, sodas, and chips and tacos for the young men who came in from the street corner to play the two video game machines—among them, Tomás Eduardo Daniel Gutiérrez, eighteen. Right away, the mother's eye picked him out for her daughter. Silvia Tecpoyotti was only fourteen, but life starts suddenly in the dust.

Olivia had seven daughters, with Silvia the third oldest. Olivia's husband had a brickyard across the street. When Silvia was thirteen and sleeping in a room with three of her sisters, the father had a bedroom added to the house. The father and mother moved into it, and soon Silvia announced that she didn't want to sleep with anybody anymore. She carried clothes into the vacant bedroom that was formerly her parents', shut the door, and the room became hers. Nobody thought of complaining. Silvia was a girl who with one long glance got everything she wanted. To make it permanent, Silvia had a lock put on the door. Such luxury, a bedroom where life can be lived in privacy and thoughts can remain personal and be protected.

She put pictures on the wall of Enrique Iglesias, the singer, and her favorite movie star, Rosa Gloria Chagoyán, an actress who could sing. Silvia's favorite movie of hers was *Lola the Trucker.*

Silvia remembers hearing for the first time, at age nine, the lecture mothers gave to all daughters: "The boy must come after you. You are never to go after the boy. Better the man comes to you and talks. You do not go to them and talk. Never. Remember this all your life." This was mixed with religious instructions so that the daughters believed any act of being forward with a boy was sacrilegious.

Silvia needed no such lecture. If she had any early wild thoughts, only she would know of them and nobody else could even have the slightest notion. As for chasing a boy, that would never be her way, even if she was wounded by her stillness in the end. Who was a boy to expect her to follow him?

As the mother inspected Eduardo, Silvia was next door doing schoolwork in the small house attached to the store.

On the street corner outside Olivia's store was a group of young men. Watching from behind her counter, Olivia could see that Eduardo was not rowdy like the others. He was tall and everybody else was short. He already had a thin mustache and brickyard arms. But he fought with nobody on the corner outside. She knew that he worked for his father in the brickyard right up the street, worked hard, and that spoke for the future more than any other quality that could be found in San Matías.

The mother didn't talk much to Eduardo. She watched and listened. To her, there was no question that he was the best of the bunch outside the store.

She told her daughter Silvia, fourteen but almost fifteen, that Eduardo was good. Silvia was the rare one who made it to junior high school. But it was still time to tell her this. Silvia was old enough to start thinking of marrying and having children. And her bright body would bring the proudest young Mexican male crawling at her feet. Oh, she would attract many young men, the daughter would, just with her eyes alone, eyes that widened in laughter and then crinkled in joy and thrilled a boy at a glance.

Then there were moments when her look reflected wisdom so far beyond a teenager. Even the young men who would have recognized intelligence were unable to sense the wisdom, for their attention was taken up by her long, curving neck, a neck as soft as a cloud. They had to remind themselves to breathe.

Silvia had seen Eduardo before, at town dances. She danced and watched him stay against the wall as if nailed to it. At this time, Teresa Hernández was the girlfriend of José Luis Bonilla. One of her sisters married Gustavo Ramirez, who lived on the dirt street behind Eduardo in San Matías. Her other sister married Alejandro Huitzil, who wanted to be an upholsterer in Puebla. It was Gustavo who started it all by leaving his wife and child and crawling into America where there were construction jobs at the astounding pay of $6 and $7 an hour in Williamsburg, in Brooklyn, where there was a builder, Ostreicher, who was going to build many buildings on streets called Lorimer and, later, just around the corner, on Middleton.

THE CITY OF NEW YORK FIRE DEPARTMENT

1ST ALARM—PHONE (STRUCT)

02/06/96 E230 E209 L102 L119 BC 35 E216 RES

03 RC01 RS04

    BOX 0341

    LORIMER STREET MARCY AVENUE

    STRUCTURAL BUILDING COLLAPSE

Found cause to be partial collapse of metal beams and building material at a new construction of homes from uppermost floors to cellar with two construction workers who were not injured, Henry Korl, mw39, and Thadeusz Sokilski, mw56. No further construction was permitted until arrival of Department of Buildings. Inspector Migone, Dept. of Buildings, arrived on the scene later. Richard Ostreicher of Industrial Enterprises which is constructing the buildings was on scene.

John M. Dillon, time arrived 9:01.

CHAPTER FOUR

In San Matías, Silvia Tecpoyotti and other young women, like Teresa Hernández, knew that you can get $4 an hour for scrubbing floors in Texas, and even more, as much as $5, for making up beds in a motel. How were they going to stay in San Matías? They were not. They believed in the Job. The young of San Matías lived their lives with pictures of American money in their heads.

One night in San Matías, Eduardo came to the corner by the store. He had his black baseball cap pulled down, but the corners of his eyes had the look of a hungry bird as they seized on Silvia's face. Inside the store, she looked out.

He walked on with his face showing nothing.

For his next visit, he came into the store with three or four of his cousins. He went right to one of the video game machines as if she were not in the place, and began manipulating the knobs.

It gave Silvia a chance to inspect his broad back, which came down in a V, and the arms shaped by carrying all those stacks of bricks for so long now.

He finished playing, and as he left with his cousins, she remem-

17

bers, he glanced at her, his eyes flicking like a camera shutter, maybe committing the sight to memory forever.

And then immediately his expression turned blank with shyness.

The following night, Eduardo's cousin Rafael came into the store.

"Eduardo thinks you are pretty," he said.

Silvia's expression was impassive.

"He told us that last night when we left here," Rafael said.

"Why doesn't he tell me himself?"

"He is afraid," Rafael said.

Silvia didn't answer, and Rafael left.

Anything Eduardo earned in the brickyard was turned over to his family. He did an adult's work and brought the money home like a kid bringing change back from going to the store. To get money for the dances, he went through the farms on the outskirts of the dusty streets and ripped up tomatoes, apples, corn, and other plants and sold them to housewives for a few pesos. Others began calling him Chato, meaning "pug nose." Afterward, virtually everybody drank fat beers and tequilas. Eduardo drank only a little. Then on the way home he unscrewed all the streetlight bulbs.

On another night, Eduardo was back in the store with two cousins, the brothers Moisés and Rafael. Now and then he would turn and look at Silvia and she would meet his eyes with a steady pleasant gaze but show him nothing more. He finished the game and left with his cousins.

Moisés had a girlfriend and was busy thinking of her. Rafael had nobody and thus became the excited messenger.

When Silvia came home from school the next day, she stopped in the store. In from the dusty street came Rafael.

"Why did you hurt Eduardo last night?"

"What?"

"You didn't talk to him. He went home saying how much he loved you and that it is sad you wouldn't speak to him."

"Why didn't he speak to me?"

"It is very hard for him. He didn't think it would be hard for you. He wants you to be his girlfriend."

By telling this to Rafael, whose brother confirmed the conversations, Eduardo was trying so clumsily to conform to the San Matías custom in which the boy must announce to all he knows that a particular girl is his girlfriend. This is an outgrowth of the old Spanish customs, Mayan suspicions, and the Catholic Church's banns of marriage. Before the boy in San Matías makes such an announcement, he cannot take the girl out alone and most certainly cannot kiss her.

Silvia thought of Eduardo's painfully shy mother walking past the store.

"Tell him to try," she said in a prayer. "Tell him for me that I like him."

Eduardo came back with three or four cousins, and they clustered around the video game machine. He never looked up. As they were leaving, he waited until his cousins were out the door, then stood in the doorway and gave a low whistle.

At first Silvia was irritated and dismissed this whistle with a wave of her hand. Then, deciding that she didn't want to chase him away forever, she smiled at him and turned away, with the long locks of her hair waving. An old woman and a young girl came in to buy crayons, she recalls, and when she finished with them, Eduardo was gone. Instantly, she missed him. The next morning, going to school, she decided that she loved the store when he was in it.

One night the next week, when Eduardo and his cousins came into the store, she suddenly felt a tap on her head. It was Eduardo. He acted as if he hadn't touched her.

"That was you," she said to him.

"No, it wasn't."

"I can tell it was you," she said.

"How could you?"

"I know who it was," she said.

But he could only fool with her when all the cousins were there. When he came in alone, it was as if his mother's blue scarf came out of the air and covered his face. He did not talk.

Then one night when it grew late and Eduardo had not been in, she found herself becoming anxious. She looked out the door and asked Rafael, "Is Eduardo coming?"

He shrugged.

"I thought he would come here," she remembers saying. The next day, another cousin, Rafael, came by. "Eduardo is so happy that you love him," he said.

"Who says that?" she said.

"That you told that to my brother Moisés last night that you love him and will die if he does not come to see you."

"Did I say that?"

"Moisés says you did. He told that to Eduardo. Eduardo is very happy. He is proud that you are his girlfriend and that you love him. He loves you."

"He should come and talk to me himself."

"Eduardo said you know."

"You tell him that I am nobody's girlfriend until I am asked."

She sent Rafael off with that directive and also with a pang in her heart.

She remembers that so well. "I loved it when he was in the store. I felt sad when he was not," she says.

She heard about a job in a hair salon in Cholula, whose streets begin only a walk away from her home. She went to the hair salon and was hired. The hours were from 4 P.M. until 9 P.M., six days a week, at 200 pesos a week, $20 a week. Come back in ten years and the hours and money are the same. She listened to the woman in charge telling everybody what to do, and she did not like it. The job put one ambition in her: She was going to get money from working in America and send it all home for a new house next to her mother's and have her own hair salon on the first floor.

In this vision, she saw Eduardo coming home from work to this house. He climbs out of a huge truck that delivers bricks. He owns the truck and he owns the brickyard. He got the money for his business by working in the United States with her.

She rushed home at day's end, so she wouldn't miss Eduardo.

On one of these nights, after she had left the store, Eduardo and his cousins Rafael and Moisés came to her house. Eduardo asked Silvia's older sister for permission to talk to Silvia.

When Silvia came out, he said, "Color our hair blond." The town style for young men was to have a blond streak in front, a rooster streak. Eduardo and the cousins felt like outsiders without it.

"Why ask me?" she remembers saying.

"Because you know how to do it."

She got out bleach and color and started on Eduardo first. He couldn't wait to look like a blond rooster.

Silvia ran her fingers through his hair. He wriggled at the touch.

"I can't do it if you don't stay still," she said.

He tried to brace himself. She could not resist drawing her fingertips across the nape of his neck. He shivered.

Now she started to bleach his hair. She had the coloring in a cup and she brushed it into his hair.

She ran her fingers lightly over his neck.

He made a sound.

But the most resonant sound came from the doorway where her father, Cristino, was watching with rising apprehension.

"Get me coffee," he said.

Silvia indicated that she was working.

"I want coffee," the father said.

Silvia had to stop and went to the small stove and heated coffee and gave it to her father, who sat on a chair like it was a guard tower.

"Why does he want his hair like this?"

"All the boys want it."

"Why do you do it for him?"

"He asks."

"Is he going to pay you?"

"No."

He asked Moisés and Rafael, "You pay her?"

They were uncomfortable but said no.

"Then why should you do it?" the father said to Silvia. *"Comida."*
He wanted to eat.

She held out her hands to show the bleach and color still on them.
He waved that off. *"Comida."*

She rushed through Eduardo's rooster streak and told the other
two that she would be right out. She went to the stove, where earlier she had made chicken and vegetables for her father.

She heard him say to Eduardo, "What time do you have to
be home?"

"Eleven," Eduardo said.

"It is late now," the father said.

Eduardo's two cousins grunted. They would go another day
without the rooster streak.

That night was the start of the father's fifteen-minute policy.

If Silvia or any of his other daughters was outside at night for
more than fifteen minutes, he called out, "What are you doing out
there? What are you talking to them about? Come in here and tell
me what you are saying to them."

To Silvia, who was openly taken with Eduardo, thus drawing the
father's sharpest attention, he said, "Here, you. Come in and make
me coffee."

As she served him, she remembers him telling her, "You can talk
a little while with a boy. Fifteen minutes. That is the most. Then you
come in."

What he didn't know was that her ears were filled only with
Eduardo's silence.

Over the months, the father's crossness waned. The desire to have his daughters fluttering around him lessened as he considered their futures and realized what every other family in San Matías did: that while it was sad to have children go away, it still was not as painful as having them all at the dinner table with truncated futures.

Always, a coyote—a smuggler—named Manuel was around the corner like a cab driver, collecting money from somebody who wanted to go to America through the Tijuana border. There were others around, walking the streets of the run-down section and onto the narrow, crowded shop streets. There was Angel, whose connections took you through Sonora to Tucson, and Pedro, whose route was through Matamoros and into Brownsville, Texas. They had unlimited customers. Virtually none of the young in these towns around Puebla thought of any future except going to America. So many people told Silvia that a chambermaid job in America was far better than what she had.

One night, she had a dream in which she was on a bus with her uncle going to the border and America, her hand gripping the back of the seat in front of her to ease the rocking. The next night she had the same dream.

Suddenly her father said to Silvia, "I know you think of going to America."

Of course she had thought of this, but it was for sometime ahead, and here the father was stating it as imminent. As long as he had brought it up, she would start planning. She waved a hand in the air, and it brushed against the new house she was building with the hair salon on the first floor.

Silvia's mother said that her brother, Silvia's uncle, had decided to go to America and if Silvia wanted to go, this would be her only chance for a long time. She would not be allowed to go on such an adventure with strangers. The uncle had arranged with the coyote Pedro to take them on his route through Matamoros and on to Brownsville. Her uncle had a brother and two nieces in College Station, Texas, where there were many motels and fast-food restaurants that needed Mexicans.

The date was set for Sunday.

Immediately, Silvia told Rafael, the messenger of romance, that she was going to America on Sunday. When Eduardo didn't come into the store that night, she shrugged, as if to shuck Eduardo off. She and a sister, Emilia, talked about a farewell outing on Saturday night at a dance concert in the stadium in Puebla. Silvia's favorite group, Bryndis, was appearing. On Friday night, they were talking about this again when Eduardo walked in with his cousins. Hearing the talk about the concert, he said to Emilia, "Can I come with you?"

Emilia said to him, "Okay. You go with her," meaning Silvia.

She never expected him on Saturday night. Her sister had set 8:30 as the time they all were to leave for the dance, and when that time came around and Eduardo was not there, she got ready to go out with her sisters.

She didn't know that Eduardo had been outside for a half hour, walking up the block, talking to people, then coming back nervously.

Finally, he was about to knock on the door just as it opened and the sisters bumped into him.

"It is a good idea that you don't go to the dance alone," her father said.

Silvia remembers that she and Eduardo stood in the doorway with her father, and they were a sentence away from being officially together.

Eduardo did not say it, but it was obvious that he had nothing else on his mind.

"I wore a tiny black blouse, a white jacket over it, and white pants," she remembers. She still can see Eduardo in black pants, a white pullover sweater, and his favorite black baseball cap.

The music the group played was slow and the lyrics romantic, and she was surprised and elated when Eduardo, with no shyness, held her close to him as they danced. She remembers pouring her body over his.

"Are you happy that I'm dancing with you?" he asked her.

"Yes," she murmured.

"I am happy," he said.

Some numbers later, still dancing close, he announced with passion, "I am happy I am dancing with you."

"And I am, too."

She was sure that the next thing he said would be a proposal, at least to be his girlfriend. Instead he fell silent. He held her tight but said nothing. The last dance was at 2 A.M. There was a large crowd and only one exit gate, and it took a long time to get through it. Silvia's sister and her boyfriend and Eduardo and Silvia were up against each other in the big crowd, and now Silvia felt that this would do it—you could see that he was thrilled to be so close to her, as was she.

They got out of the park and into a cab. She sat and waited for him to suggest a stop. The cab went up to her house, next to the store. Her sister and her boyfriend got out. Silvia did not move. Of course he was going to kiss her.

When he did not move for many moments, she got out of the cab.

He waved at her as the cab pulled away.

The next morning, she stood on the street for a moment.

"What are you doing there?" her mother said. "Your uncle won't be here for a half hour."

"I know," she said.

She waited in that dusty street, and when Eduardo did not come up it, she was about to break all the rules of her life and go down to that brickyard and maybe the moment he saw her he would come over and hold her, the way he had when they had danced the night before, and he would tell her that he wanted her to be his girlfriend and then she would say to her uncle, no, you go, I am staying here because I love Eduardo.

"Are you ready?" she remembers hearing her uncle say.

This was on the morning of May 8, 1998.

CHAPTER FIVE

Silvia was going into a world where the two American faiths rule at once, and people like her die because they cannot tell the difference.

There is the American worship of commerce that piles money to the sky and makes all good people rich. This moves in the opposite direction of an older belief, one whose prayer books still carry the smell of cold winter seawater from the wood ships of the Puritans, who came to run the morals of a nation. All these years later, their teachings that dourness is good and laughter is bad still cause Washington to make the control of strangers of great importance. If they are not white, then they come from the devil.

There was an afternoon in the House of Representatives in Washington when Peter King watched warily as Rick Lazio walked toward him.

King, a Republican congressman from Long Island, was standing in the aisle and Lazio, then another Republican congressman from Long Island, came on an errand on behalf of the Speaker of the House of Representatives, Newt Gingrich. It was over a bill that would allow immigrants without papers to be deported, right at the airport if found there, with no hearings. Tackle them in airports and at borders, tie them up, and send them back like packages. No hearing or evidence would be required.

"The Speaker wants to know what we need to do for your support in the future," Lazio said.

"Don't bring around any more bills like this," King said.

The bill was sponsored by Lamar Smith, a Republican congressman from Texas, a state that resents and reviles all Mexicans, although they will hire them for $3 an hour. It was cosponsored by Alan Simpson, then a Republican senator from Wyoming, which had 430,000 residents at the time and enough room for the population of a couple of countries.

One part of the bill said that "secret evidence" was allowed at immigration hearings. The phrase brought on an ancient fury in King, who had been all through this during his struggles to get a travel visa for Gerry Adams, the Catholic leader from Northern Ireland. King wanted him to speak to the American Irish. The State Department said there was "classified evidence" that Adams was a danger. They said that they owed it to the British government to keep Adams out. It took years for King to get the decision overturned, during which time his distrust became permanent. Now, on this day in Washington, King stood in the Congress of the United States and looked at the phrase "secret evidence." He saw it as un-American. He voted no. And he would vote no on any other immigration bill of its kind.

Later, walking back to his office across the street from the Capitol, he was saying, "It comes out to be fear, I guess. The idea of a bunch of Mexicans walking around the country—it frightens them. If you ask any questions about immigration, nobody has an answer. They feel it is something so bad that you don't have to explain it."

Now the names have changed. Gingrich of Georgia made everybody furious. Then his moral purity was slightly marred by one girlfriend and he was out. Suddenly, about to take his place is

Robert Livingston from Louisiana, a sure antiterrorist. He wanted executions of immigrant terrorists, and if they weren't caught with a bomb, the gas chamber still would do. Livingston is on the floor of the House, about to be voted Speaker of the House. He decides to display his dislike for President Clinton. He calls over to the Democratic side that President Clinton should resign because he is an immoral pig with a girlfriend, Monica. The Democrats rise and shriek, "You resign! You resign!" They are telling each other the news that Livingston has four girlfriends. He has them in motels. Livingston happens to glance upward. He sees two of his four girlfriends. "Motel Livingston!" people shout. "You resign! You resign!!"

"All right, I will," he says. He walks off the floor. His chief supporters run to the back to pick a successor, Dennis Hastert. This one doesn't know Irish without papers or a Mexican. The whip, Rick Lazio, soon is gone. He is replaced by Tommy Reynolds from New York, whose field of interest is Niagara Falls.

And nothing changes. Peter King still goes to his seat ready to oppose any and all bills. None comes up.

Motel Livingston now stalks Capitol Hill as a lobbyist for Turkey. Somebody in the House is sponsoring a resolution condemning Turkey for slaughtering Armenians in 1915, and Livingston is hired to block it. "Turkey is not for genocide," he says. The trucks running through the border towns, carrying mufflers from Mexico and television sets from California, have superseded visions of terrorists or of most any other deaths in Congress. Money wins again.

And in Mexico a new president is worried about immigrants coming into southern Mexico from Guatemala and Honduras. For the northern border he sees a program of guest workers, and Mexican farm labor groups in the United States squall that under this, a guest worker would not be allowed to join an American labor union. "Ensured slavery!" they shout.

Once, virtually all Mexican immigrants made it into the United States safely. At El Paso, the entrance was made from the *colonias*, the shantytowns as hideous as anything in places like Rio or Rwanda, on the edge of the city of Juárez. This was accomplished by fording the shallow brown water of the Rio Grande. Many coming from Juárez who didn't want to come up the river so far took the "ferry," an inner tube pulled by rope across the river, which was wide at this point. The border agents were up on the bridge between Juárez and El Paso, guarding the United States border.

The largest number took the obvious path through Tijuana. They came off the planes on Rodriguez Field, where the air was filled with the magical sound of the song of America, cars rushing, truck horns blaring, smaller and insistent car horns, all of it on U.S. Highway 35, visible from out there on the runways. You can see the American road! The road ran from the large customs and immigration border inspection station at San Ysidro, just yards away, with twin plaques marking the borders of each country. The border is marked on the roadway pavement by a twin line of small metal nipples running across the twenty-four lanes. A dozen southbound lanes go to Mexico, and another dozen lanes go up the coast to San Diego, only miles away, and on to Los Angeles, to the airports, to all of America, to New York. From Rodriguez Field, they slipped through the bushes and across the sand leading up to the highway. Usually, they gathered at 4 P.M., at the changing of shifts of the American border guards, whose schedule they knew as if it were a town prayer. They had only to go over a weak wire fence with barbed wire at the top, barbed wire that could be nullified by one jacket draped over it. Then the whole pack would go up and over; it could be a couple of hundred, suddenly sprinting across the border line wherever you looked, and with speedy little strides covering twelve lanes to the center divider, a step over that, and another run for life and riches across twelve more lanes to the other side. The Mexicans who made it across the highway were new Americans. They melded in with the residents of the apartments and started walking toward San Diego as if they were heading for a store around the corner.

Frequently there was the shriek of brakes and the bare lights of emergency workers; a Mexican, crumpled like a piece of paper, was dead on the highway. Month after month, the Mexicans came off the airport runways. Night after night, Mexican after Mexican went high into the air as they were hit by a car, a trailer truck. So many that Jesus Garcia, the state of California's transportation director, erected a twelve-foot-high heavy wire fence on the highway divider to make it impossible for anybody to get across and be killed while making their run for America.

This way of crossing a border ended with the wave of a gun. A force of nineteen thousand Border Patrol guards spread across the Southwest, from San Diego through Nogales and Douglas in Arizona and Laredo and Brownsville and Corpus Christi in Texas. The towns carry the names of famous western stories, most of which never happened or, if anything did, one shot in real life became a thousand in cheap western stories or preposterous movies.

At the crossing to San Diego, the records of combined forces showed that they turned back 524,231 Mexicans. About a million made it through. Near the end of 1999, they had for the single year stopped 182,267, which seems like a tremendous victory, except three still got through for every one stopped. Yet it still was a gamble for a Mexican to try without a professional smuggler—a coyote.

Suddenly, and from everywhere, the traffic became overwhelming. The North American Free Trade Agreement of January 1, 1994, erased duties and left customs and immigration people standing at ramparts designed to inspect and impound drugs and keep out Mexicans without papers, trying to block a flood with their feet. All border troops try to ignore being parties to the fiction that you can stop masses of people who want to move. They stand on the border as fierce defenders of the American way of life: paycheck. And as part of the great new law enforcement industry, they understand the need for official statistics. Stop two illegals, the figure becomes five in a government press release in Washington.

This still requires a lot of plain hard, frustrating work. They'll receive a tip that a trailer truck is coming through with illegals. Stop the truck and find sixty Mexicans huddled in back. Send them back. Away goes the truck. Acting on information and belief, agents pull over a van and find many pounds of marijuana. The driver says he has no idea how it got there. He is arrested. And as far as the eye can see there is a line of trucks waiting to cross, eighteen-wheel trailer trucks coming from Tijuana. An average of three thousand trailer trucks brush past the border booths every twenty-four hours like an armored column and head anywhere in America.

And in the southbound lanes, another three thousand trucks head from America to Mexico.

Some American unions said the safety standards of these Mexican trucks and their drivers was so low that they were a rolling threat to America. That never happened. The California Highway Patrol and the local San Diego police could not come up with any records of an uncommon number of trucks from Mexico, or trucks going there, involved in accidents on Highway 35. By May of 2000, the Senate Commerce Committee found that of the 63,000 trucks from Mexico running in the United States, 73 percent were inspected during the year and therefore rated as approved.

The common fear was that trucks from Mexico carrying cheaply produced goods would suck up the American economy.

"I don't see anything sucked up," Rudy Camacho, the customs agent in charge of southern California, said as he stood at the border plaza, the sound of trucks forcing him to keep his voice raised. "One can't do without the other anymore. Twenty billion dollars a year in trade. Southern California can't do without it. What's it done to Mexico? It woke up a sleeping giant."

Ray Kelly, then customs commissioner, in for a visit from Washington, stood at the Tijuana crossing and watched the long lines of trailer trucks. Once he figured out that the ones coming from Mexico were carrying mufflers for America, thousands of mufflers, he knew the idea of stopping Mexico was over. "You get something this commonly used and if you slow it up, you'll have auto dealers calling for your head," he said. "What's happened is we've been overwhelmed. The government agencies can't handle the situation. We all need more people. We're told to forget it. What they want is more roads to handle all this. We seized three hundred eighty-five thousand pounds of drugs this year. Pot. We're burning forty thousand pounds of it tomorrow in Long Beach. I don't care how you feel about drugs or pot, but nobody in Washington is interested in drugs anymore. Whether anybody wants to recognize it or not, we're going to have more and more trouble stopping drugs from coming through. Who knew there would be this many trucks?" Nor a war.

The immigrants don't have the complicated daily life of a drug carrier. The drug carriers risk millions and millions. They could lose their freedom and frequently even their lives. They have enemies when they leave and enemies when they arrive.

Immigrants have to risk danger, and more of them die crossing the border, and the prize is the chance to go to work for below minimum wage and be lonely in America.

EDUARDO'S FATHER REMEMBERS that a most improbable man named Chockaloo was the first to leave San Matías for the United States.

"Why go there?" he remembers asking Chockaloo.

"Trabajo."

"You don't even work *here,*" Daniel said.

Reluctantly, many of the men in town donated something and wished Chockaloo great luck. Some even thought he was brave. Nobody they knew had ever done this. Daniel recalls kissing him goodbye. He was off to America, facing a new life with only the clothes he was wearing, a shirt and pants.

The owner of a grocery store on the main road outside of San Matías told Daniel that Chockaloo bought several bottles of beer and drank them on the roadside while waiting for the airport van. He drank enough beer to allow him to open a bottle of tequila that he had also bought. Later, off into the sky went Chockaloo. As he had never been higher than the roof of a brickyard shack, the alcohol was the only thing that kept him on the plane.

Some months later, Chockaloo's mother was at the money order window in the appliance store—stoves, television, sound systems—in Cholula, asking if anything had arrived for her. She got what she expected—nothing,

"Mama, Chockaloo is home!" a nephew shouted as she came back to her house. Here suddenly was her most wonderful son back in the house.

"He told everybody that the police beat him in New York and he couldn't work," Daniel says.

He sat on street corners and told everybody of his trip to the United States. He did not know that daily Tijuana bristled with more new, young, eager, heavily armed law enforcement agents and that no longer could you merely run across a highway. The most expensive coyotes were needed.

Chockaloo had no idea of this. He had gone through Tijuana. He thought that made him a sage. He told Eduardo that crossing the border at Tijuana was the same as walking across Calle Libre. He told Eduardo that he stood on the first street of Tijuana, at a drugstore painted blue that sold coffee, and was at the exact edge of the highway, only yards away from the United States line, and that everybody in front of the store used the outdoor pay booths to call people and tell them what they were seeing, that their car just passed through the inspection plaza, and when there would be a change of shift for the guards.

There is no way of knowing how many young people listened

to Chockaloo on the street corner, bought him a bottle of beer, and then went up to Tijuana and were terrorized by the guns of border guards and thrown back like refuse. Silvia's uncle told her that if she wished to be eaten by animals in the desert or thrown in jail in the United States, then she should listen to Chockaloo or anybody else in town. "I will take you. If they say Tijuana, we'll go the other way."

The fences at Tijuana were erected by a government that doesn't know the history of the last twenty minutes.

There was a night in Berlin in 1989 when crowds cheered in the damp night air for each sledgehammer that thudded into the Berlin Wall. And two women who took their first subway ride out of East Berlin in twenty-eight years came up the steps in West Berlin. The commercials of the West had drifted over the wall and into the taste buds of the people on the desolate streets of East Berlin.

They were astonished by the blinding neon of democracy. Right away, one of them said: "Ah, look. Burger King."

And as if Berlin had never happened, the United States government boasts that it has a wall that can keep out millions who have watched since they were first able to see a ceaseless rainfall of American diamond chips on their television.

No matter. The federal immigration people were enthralled by the sight of the highway fence at San Ysidro. Right away, they erected a double corrugated metal fence along the border that was high enough to repel an immigrant trying to cross on a cherry picker. The fence sits like a dreary surprise to somebody turning a corner on the streets of the freight center at Otay Mesa, which is a minute or two from the border gates at San Ysidro. The tan metal has a deadening effect on the commercial street. Light towers like those usually found at a ballpark rise over the fence, and at night their harsh, ominous glare makes a prison wall seem soft. A white Border Patrol car with an agent is on the street. Another car sits on an embankment and is almost flush against the fence. The fence runs for 180 miles with border guards said to be in sight of each other all the way. These are figures that can be checked only by going into the desert.

The Border Patrol is the most untruthful of government agencies after the White House. Even if real, these seemingly impressive statistics are out of a candy store. The border is over two thousand miles long, and enforcement at familiar places, the Tijuana crossing or one at Laredo, Texas, or Nogales, Arizona, only forces so many Mexican immigrants to walk blindly into lonely, dangerous areas where there is a river that takes lives, then miles of thorny, knee-high scrub running up to the mountains and then farther out, into the bare hot lands of Arizona and New Mexico and Texas, a desert that is the basement floor of the earth.

CHAPTER SIX

Silvia left San Matías with her uncle and took several buses that crawled to Matamoros, on the Gulf of Mexico, across the Rio Grande from Brownsville, Texas. By now there were five who had paid for the coyote. They checked into the Fontana Hotel for $400 for the one room and remained there a day. Then there was banging on the door and a young guy of about nineteen told them they were leaving immediately. The price for walking from the border with a guide to Houston was $600, and Silvia was told the trip would take fifteen days. They were stacked atop of each other in a taxi like luggage. Piling out at the edge of the town, they followed the coyote into high weeds that turned into hot red dirt with low thorny bushes.

Silvia remembers that the coyote yelled, "Run," and they ran, then "Walk," and when they had their breaths back, they ran again. Silvia congratulated herself for bringing a minimum of clothes in the small suitcase, for there was no way of carrying anything heavy. She thinks they ran and walked for five hours, until suddenly the next step was into a ditch, at the bottom of which was the river, narrow— the water dark and seemingly shallow and seemingly innocent. A stick on the surface was moving quickly enough to indicate a strong current. Silvia took off her sneakers and held them high over her head with the suitcase. Then she went barefoot into the water. At this point in the nineteen-hundred-mile-long Rio Grande, the water is shallow and the current deceptive. Then the river can widen and rise until it is sixty feet deep and cold, with a current strong enough to carry a house away. At all times, it is treacherous for young Mexicans, whose experience with water is usually limited to a bucket in a well.

On this day, Silvia listed herself as sixteen, but she was still a little short of that. She had no experience in water, but went into the river with the nerves of a trained guerrilla. The river bottom was sand. Each small step brought her deeper, until the water was up to her neck. She remembers that the current pushed hard on the back of her ankles and lifted her heels and curled under her toes and tried to yank her feet from the sand, turning her into part of the current. Her uncle remembers the strength of the current taking him by surprise. Silvia had strong and limber legs that secured her footing. She dug her toes in and took one step at a time, holding one foot in the sand as an anchor, and soon each step was firmer and took her upper body out of the water.

Many become paralyzed with sudden fear and go off their feet and drown in three feet of water. Any page of any record of the United States Border Patrol has columns filled with lists such as this:

NAME	COUNTY	CAUSE OF DEATH
Unknown	Maverick	Drowning
Unknown	Maverick	Drowning
Unknown	Uvalde	Unknown
Unknown	Kinney	Drowning
Jeronimo Mendoza Guzman	Zavala	Drowning

Del Rio Patrol Sector

NAME	COUNTY	CAUSE OF DEATH
Raul Martínez Delgado	Maverick	Exposure—Heat
Unknown	Maverick	Exposure—Heat

Raul Albarran	Maverick	Exposure—Heat
Unknown	Maverick	Exposure—Heat
Unknown	Dimmit	Unknown
Jorge Cabrera Tovar	Uvalde	Exposure—Heat
Unknown	Kinney	Unknown

Silvia and the group were now in Kenedy County, Texas, and in fact on the Kenedy Ranch, 230,000 acres of mesquite and sandy soil and emptiness, in whose hollows were sometimes found the bleached bones of those who have tried to hide from the sun. She wore two pairs of jeans to protect against the snakes that coiled across the land. These snakes are mostly diamondback rattlers as thick as a fuel hose.

They walked at night, starting at 9 P.M. These were old trails. Often there would be a warning sound from the coyote leading them, and they would promptly fall onto the dirt and, looking up, see a Border Patrol wagon jouncing along.

Somewhere in the night, Silvia was on the ground when the guy nearest her made a motion with his hand. Silvia heard the snake, a hissing sound as it moved over the dirt. If she stood and ran from it, the Border Patrol would see her and probably all the others, and they would be sent back to Mexico—and she was not here to be in Mexico. If she stayed down, the snake could be on her. It was the same as all the other snakes, but it hissed rather than its tail rattling like a gourd. Was it so much closer? The patrol wagon rocked and roared. Was it ever going to get farther away?

"I got ready to kick at the snake," she remembers. "That is all I could do."

Soon the Border Patrol was gone, and she crawled rapidly away from the snake.

Sometime later they came to railroad tracks that suddenly appeared in the mesquite. There were no signs or gates or poles. Just railroad tracks in the emptiness of the night.

"These are good," somebody said. "Snakes don't go on tracks. We'll stay on these for a while."

Records of the county coroner show that the sixth young man to die in a six-month period in Kenedy County, Texas, stopped on the railroad tracks running through the flat hot land, and he and the guy with him intended to rest with their heads on the rails. Mexicans on the trudge north believe that snakes recoil from steel tracks. Instead of resting, they fell asleep with their heads on the rail. A freight train running fast, with no crossing to worry about, no lights, no horns, roared down the tracks. One of the two on the tracks got up and fled. The other was still asleep as the train engineer tried to stop the freight, but he needed a mile for that and he cut through the young guy on the tracks like a steak knife. On another night, a mile away, on the same tracks, a train came rushing up on three who were sleeping. Two rolled away; one stayed and was left in ribbons. Then six were asleep on the tracks when a 105-car Union Pacific freight train carrying scrap metal and paper came through the night at fifty miles an hour and wiped them out. The engineer thought he saw something on the tracks, but there was no way of stopping.

The record was set at Kingsville, where forty Mexicans were walking north on a railroad trestle in the middle of a Saturday night when a train came around a curve and directly at them. Some jumped into a creek four stories down. Some tried to outrun the forty-three-car freight train. Others flattened themselves against the side of the trestle. Four died.

Silvia went on the railroad tracks, stepping from one tie to another, free of the fear of snakes and with no Border Patrol in sight. They walked that way for an hour, she remembers, and then one of them turned in the darkness. *"Tren!"* They hadn't bothered to look, and they could hear no sound even in the stillness of the night. Silvia remembers that the one big light seemed a long way off. People sauntered off the tracks. She looked as she was getting off and suddenly the light was closer. She jumped off the tracks and went down the embankment just as the train moved through a night that thwarted depth perception. Two engines raced by furiously, and behind them came freight cars whose wheels squealed as if they were being ground. She turned icy as she realized how close the train had been. And now that she was off the tracks, she had to worry about snakes again. Anything you can see that looks different is a snake, she told herself. But mostly she could not make out the ground itself and stepped blindly.

At dawn, the group stopped while the guide looked at his watch and muttered. A truck was supposed to be here, he said. They waited for two hours. Then in the first heat of morning, Silvia walked into a town with her uncle and Moisés, Eduardo's cousin, to buy food. Suddenly a white Border Patrol van came onto the street. The three crouched behind bushes—big bushes that could hide them all day, Silvia thought. Some moments later, she heard a sound alongside her. Next to her now was the polished boot of an immigration agent. Several Border Patrol cops with guns in their hands stood over them. They put Silvia, her uncle, and Moisés into the van and drove them through the border station over the small bridge across the river and threw them out in Matamoros.

"Don't ever come back or we'll put you in jail," they told her.

CHAPTER SEVEN

n San Matías and the thousand other Mexican towns where hope sits in a fading light, the young never did consider the idea of danger of going north to the United States. Their destination is the Job, not the town or city. And ahead of them, a country fearful and hateful of them has its fences up at the logical crossing points: Tijuana into San Diego on one coast, and through Nogales and Douglas in Arizona and Laredo in Texas and on into El Paso in the middle of the Southwest, where the Mexicans are pushed into the desert as if they are going through a turnstile. After that, they walk until they make it or die. They walk for the Job. There is no time to the Job. It is before all and after all.

They come across the riverbanks and the dry borderlands, these people who want to work, who want to scrub floors and clean pots, or mow lawns, or live in shacks alongside the farms they work on, or show up every day in the grimmest of factory jobs, or wash dishes in the coffee shops of the country—or work construction in Brooklyn for low wages on jobs on which white union members are paid five times as much.

And trying to get there, in all the dust from the wind and the powdered earth rising from their feet, crystals of air snap and unseen fingers high up in the dust clouds suddenly determine the fate on the ground. Nobody disputes this. It happens too often.

Bleached bones were found in the desert outside of Dateland, Arizona. A birth certificate in the sand alongside the bones identified Oscar Peña-Moreno, who had left Guasave, Sinoloa, in May 1996 with two lifelong friends. Their trip north would logically have been through El Paso, but with that town now heavily patrolled, they must have headed west. The three were married to sisters. They were not heard from again. Agents came upon the bones on December 4, 1997, and brought them to the coroner in Pima County, which is Tucson. Of course the flesh was no more. Desert hogs, coyotes, and birds had eaten all. Oscar Peña-Moreno's wallet, which contained his identification, was found in a pair of pants recovered with the bones. For some reason, the coroner cremated the bones and held them in an urn for the family. The people in Guasave pooled whatever money they had and sent the mother of Oscar Peña-Moreno and his wife, Ramona, to Tucson. She took the urn from the coroner and stood motionless with it. Then she put it down on a counter.

"This is not my son," she said.

The coroner explained that of course it was her son. Here is his birth certificate.

"This is not my son," she said.

She went back to Guasave.

Victor Chacon, who is with the federal public defender's office in Tucson, shrugged when he caught the case. This would not be the first time that something in the sky was right and everybody here was wrong. Later, the widow of Oscar Peña-Moreno, whose name is Ramona Quintero, said that of course the mother was right in refusing the ashes. "She prayed to the saint," she said. "She awaits his return. He is alive somewhere."

After which, in the matter of Peña-Moreno's ashes, he found it unsurprising to receive unrelenting pressure from the mother, who said her son and the two who had been with him were working in a logging camp in Utah.

Victor Chacon mistrusted the identification found in the desert. He stated in his report, "Illegal immigrants are often accosted by bands of robbers in remote areas. The robbers make the victims remove all of their clothing. This way the robbers know that the victims are not hiding anything of value. The coroner stated that because clothing gets mixed up, identifications are lost or wind up in other clothes. He states that he has had two cases recently in which the dead person was carrying someone else's identification."

Before the cremation, an autopsy had showed the victim had sixteen teeth in the upper jaw. Peña-Moreno's mother said that one day he had jumped on a bike and had gone to have a throbbing upper molar pulled. She didn't know the dentist. Chacon called every dentist in Peña-Moreno's area. None kept records. His phone calls and the realization that many were dying unidentified have now caused dentists to begin keeping records. However, a woman dentist said that she remembered taking the molar from Peña-Moreno's upper jaw. There was no evidence of any missing molar in the remains examined in Tucson.

The mother was right. The sky had told her so.

For Silvia and the others from San Matías, their being women didn't hinder them from attempting the crossing. The tragedy of the border could be seen on the television now and then, but not enough to stop them. There were only some distinctions that caused special attention: a pregnancy or a babe in arms. Otherwise, women went walking the same as men under a pitiless sun that raises temperatures to 140 degrees.

THE NURSE STANDS in the hospital in Bisbee with a hand on the little boy's shoulder as he sits on the examining table. The boy's feet dangle in muddy ripped little tennis shoes.

A nurse looks at the thin man in the doorway, sees his bleak look, and says nothing. He has on a short-sleeved shirt and tie.

The man has been trying to think of something he can do for this kid, and when he sees these ripped and muddy tennis shoes he tells himself, new shoes.

Now he hears people coming along the hall, and his mind out-races the sound of their feet. He knows exactly what it means, and he doesn't want to deal with it. At sixty-five, Miguel Escobar Valdez, the Mexican consul in Douglas, Arizona, has been everywhere for his government. He was in Chicago when they reassigned him here. He is calm enough to be helpful at a moment like this, in this room in the Copper Queen Hospital in Bisbee, the next town up from Douglas, a town of a few empty streets that are the last ones in America.

He is here because this little boy, Carlos Bacan, five, started out ten days ago with his eleven-year-old sister, Ana-Laura Bacan, and their mother, Rosalia Bacan Miranda, thirty-three, from the town of Coacoalco, outside of Mexico City. At 10:30 in the morning of the tenth day they were walking for the long last day before reaching the border, which was forty miles away. Two days earlier, they were in Agua Prieta, a Mexican town that is on the other side of a fence, and one pace in the sand, across the border from Douglas. The fence and the Border Patrol agents at Douglas force people to walk far out into the desert to go around the fortifications. The mother and children were trudging with two neighbors from their home-town. The boy could not keep up with the adults, and neither could his mother, who moaned as she lifted her foot for another step. The neighbors said they were going ahead to see if any Border Patrol agents were around. They said they would return to Rosalia and her children. Sure they would. When the sand turned to snow. They walked off. They left the mother and two children to suffer through hours of hot dirt and the sweeping bitter fields of unyielding knee-high thorn bushes. In the distance on three sides, dark mountains crowded into clouds. Ahead was a sky the color of heat. The mother, Rosalia, had brought only a large bottle of water; most of it was gone, and though she was dehydrated, she took only tiny gulps of water and gave the rest to her children.

The blood of an adult at all times needs five to six liters of water, and when there is less, the vessels contract, the kidneys become dangerously inactive and simultaneously the heart deals with less blood for all the body. Sometime soon, the problem is solved by either fluid or death.

That day it was about 110 degrees everywhere, but out in the desert, where the land throws off heat that mixes with the rays of the sun, the temperature is measured by what it does to people. Rosalia sat, then tumbled full-length into the red sand. Her breathing came from a strangled throat. The daughter tried to give her water, but the mother said no. Her hand waved weakly. You and the boy take the water. She passed out.

The daughter thought she had fainted. She shook the last drops of water onto the mother's cracked lips. The mother didn't respond and the water dripped from her lips. Ana-Laura told her brother to stay with the mother. She walked through thorn bushes until she came to a brown rutted road. She saw and heard nothing. Suddenly, a gas company truck came along and pulled over. The driver called the Border Patrol.

At the hospital, somebody called the Mexican consul, Miguel Escobar Valdez, in his office in Douglas. Now he is standing in the doorway to this first-floor room at Copper Queen Hospital in Bisbee, gathering himself for the sounds coming down the hall.

The girl, Ana-Laura, walks alongside the doctor. She is short and very dark. Her eyes are dry and fixed straight ahead. She has on a T-shirt and jeans. The tennis shoes are caked with mud.

The consul is going to say something to her as she passes, but he does not. I know this one in my heart, he tells himself. She will do this her way.

Ana-Laura stands in front of the brother, whose legs dangle from the examining table.

"*Mama murio*," she tells the little face.

Escobar sees that the boy doesn't understand.

"*Mama murio*," Ana-Laura tells the boy again.

He shows nothing.

She leans to him and whispers.

The boy moves just this little bit.

She leans forward again and whispers.

Does he nod?

I am not about to get near her, Escobar tells himself. The nurse and doctor keep their distance. They understand that these are sacred murmurings, not for their ears.

The girl steps back and looks steadily and solemnly at Escobar.

She has told her brother that the mother is dead. Now what would you have me do?

She says to the brother, "*Ven para aca.*" Come over here.

He slides off the table and stands next to her. She walks over to Escobar. The boy is with her. The boy looks at her, expecting a decision from her. Now she is the mother.

Escobar asks her where she is from and for the names of her relatives, and the girl tells him that he must call her aunt in her hometown. The girl has the phone number memorized.

The nurses show them a table of food in another room. The boy sits down and eats. The girl wants only iced tea and then drinks only some of it.

In the town where they come from, people collected money to send the uncle to Douglas. The consulate paid for the mortuary dressing of the mother, and she is now being shipped home. The uncle and two children go across the border to the shabby bus station at Agua Pietra for the long ride to Hermosillo, and a plane to Mexico City and home.

Escobar stands at the bus as the family gets on. He pats the boy. Now the eleven-year-old girl, with the demeanor of a diplomat, steps up to him and shakes hands. She thanks him for their new tennis shoes.

Escobar throws his arms around the girl and hugs her.

When he lets her go, he is crying.

She is not. Her eleven-year-old face does not change. She gets on the bus.

In Douglas, at the last alley that runs off the last yards of the American side of the Pan-American Highway, there is a tan picket fence, without barbed wire at the top, that separates the last houses of Douglas and the first of Agua Prieta, Sonora. Two kids in T-shirts, twelve years old maybe, climb the fence easily on the Mexican side and then climb down into the first alley of America.

Suddenly a white immigration jeep pulls up, and a woman agent gets out and starts walking purposefully toward the kids, who now are the heart and soul of the danger to America. Illegal Mexican immigrants. Right away, when they see her, they climb the fence back to Mexico.

A second white immigration van pulls up, and another one after that.

There are six officers to answer the call on kids climbing a fence. The female agent, who has caught the case, walks toward the fence.

From the top, one of the kids cackles and gives the woman the arm. One, two, three times. Which is the only reason he went over the fence to begin with.

Now a woman holding a baby walks from a house on the American side and goes up to the fence. A man comes out of the last house on the Mexican side. He stands at the fence and the two talk through the pickets for some time.

Our country spends billions for protection from these most dangerous enemy acts.

CHAPTER EIGHT

At the heaviest center for border commerce in the country, the narrow river crossing from Nuevo Laredo in Mexico to Laredo in Texas, customs agents estimate trailer trucks account for something like $30 billion in business each year.

Immigration and Border Patrol people in the Laredo area estimate that they catch one of every eleven who scurry across the border illegally.

All those people can barely understand the barbed wire and patrols when they approach American cities in the Southwest. Back in their home villages and towns, they learn in classrooms and at dinner tables that all this land was owned by Mexico, and that the cities and rivers and mountains keep their Spanish names because they are by common law Mexican. The Rio Bravo is the river, the Sierra Madre is the mountains, and the cities are San Diego, Laredo, Nogales, Albuquerque, and El Paso. California once was Mexico. To a traveler from Mexico, these are places that cannot be so far from Mexico; the names tell you that they must be so close that they are merely places that you go to and then return. They are baffled at being hunted at the border by the helicopters and searchlights and jeeps filled with men in uniform with guns. How can you oppose my coming across your line in the sand as I go from Tijuana to San Diego, a place that once was my country and remains that way now by population alone?

The journey to Chicago and New York is the foreign experience for Mexican immigrants. These American cities have far fewer Mexican tones than the Southwest. Much more so in New York, where Mexicans aren't the dominant Hispanic group and have less history and are at the bottom of the Hispanic staircase, the foreigners of the Hispanics. They are more likely to have prominent Indian features than other Hispanics. When they come to Arizona, they feel they are walking on lands they have owned for centuries.

Still, the Border Patrol had a crackdown called Operation Hold the Line that drove people out to places where nobody with sense would dare go, into the worst of the desert.

Margarita Alvarado, thirty-two, and her brother-in-law, Juan Manuel, nineteen, walked into the plaza at Nuevo Laredo, a couple of short streets from the bridge going over the river to Laredo, Texas. The square has a fountain in the center and benches where common people sit to rest and inspect the air. They are alongside the street royalty, the young men who claim that for cash they can guide you across the river and into the land where money floats through the air.

The streets around the square are lined with open-air drugstores, some of which sell American prescription drugs at the lowest of prices and others proclaiming "Farmacia Express," meaning all you want of what you want.

Strolling into the square are people in dresses and tight jeans, some of whom might be women. The yellow and white church, Santo Niño, is on one side. Through the open door you can read a great banner hanging inside and advertising La Indulgencia Plenaria del Jubileo 2000. For the anniversary, a plenary indulgence is granted somehow. A plenary indulgence sends you through the gates of heaven as if you actually belonged.

The indulgence is believed in by most everybody, and, because of such things, the Mexicans come north with a faith that seems as deep and strict as that of the Irish.

The interior of the church in Nuevo Laredo is painted gold. In San Matías, which is even poorer and thus spends on worship until there is true pain, the pillars have many decorations of heavy gold in the form of wreaths. The gold goes to the ceiling and across it, and candlelight causes the entire church to seem to burst into small fires.

Now in Nuevo Laredo, Margarita Alvarado walked up the steps to the church, said a prayer, and returned to pay the coyote whatever she had and followed him out of town, into the desert of thorn bushes and, after that, great stretches of sand fire. Apparently they had bought one gallon of water in a store off the square. A gallon weighs nine pounds. The woman would actually need five gallons alone, but she couldn't carry forty-five pounds. Margarita risked thirst rather than trudge along with the five gallons she needed.

She got through the desert brush, in heat that made her stagger, and then she collapsed and died on the bank of the shallow narrow river.

She was another name on a roster of people who died looking for the Job.

CHAPTER NINE

Until the attack on New York, the United States believed in the word *war* as a vital part of any effort against the things troubling the country.

Lyndon Johnson had a war on poverty.

There is a war on cancer.

There is a war on illiteracy.

There was Jimmy Carter's moral equivalent of war on an oil shortage.

And there is the war on drugs.

There is a peace wing to this war. "Just say no," Nancy Reagan said with a straight face.

"We can get the job done with a helicopter gunship," promised General Barry McCaffrey when he was the nation's official drug czar.

However, the word *crusade* then came into the language and replaced *war*. All the real Crusades did was kill innocent people who believed in a different faith, but the word has lived on to imply Christian valor.

The dates of the Crusades suddenly are eerie. They were held in 1350. Muhammad appeared on or about 650. Now, 1350 years old,

Islam produces terrorists who attack America in a crusade that uses another name, just as Rome sent out its Crusaders in the year 1350.

Now we say there is an antidrug crusade.

We also have an antijaywalking crusade, a crusade against overtime in the Department of Sanitation, and personal political crusades: "I am on a crusade to become the state comptroller!"

The late Senator Paul Cloverdell, a Georgia Republican, and Representative Porter Goss, also a Republican from that state, came up with a bill that would have stopped anybody from doing business with any company that might somehow have some financial ties with a Mexican drug lord. No evidence was required. Just the presence of Mexicans.

"How can we be sure that the Mexican company doesn't have drug money invested in it?" Cloverdell was asked.

"So many of these Mexican companies," he sighed. "Well, you take these people coming across the border. How many of them do you think are carrying drugs?"

He thought the answer was just about all.

Yet for those coming from places such as San Matías, none. "Nobody uses drugs here because they don't have the money to buy them," Eduardo's father, Daniel, said one day. "It is not that we are so much better."

In the brickyard in San Matías, Eduardo was shackled with shyness. He could hardly talk to Silvia when he was in the same room with her. Talking to her on the phone might be easier, he thought. At her mother's store, he played the video machine and after it, offhandedly, he asked how Silvia was. The mother said she had not heard anything from her and that she was worried. All these stories on television about people dying trying to cross. Where was this College Station where she had gone? He had never heard of any jobs there, and that was the only way to determine where he would go. You move to the Job.

Gustavo, who lived behind him and had gone to America earlier, had called several times from Brooklyn and said he had a construction job and that the boss, Ostreicher, could use more workers. The pay was immense: Gustavo said he was making $7 an hour. Seven dollars in one hour! Eduardo carried bricks all day for the equivalent of $5 a day and talked about the money Gustavo was making in America. Hearing this, his father knew that he was about to lose a son. There was a compelling reason. Eduardo and Daniel had started to build a new two-story addition at one end of the courtyard after work, with Eduardo mixing concrete and his father and a couple of relatives digging a foundation, but the money ran out. All these things that go into putting up a building of any size— the lumber, the supports, the ironwork—cost more than they had.

Eduardo began to put money away to pay a coyote who would get him to America. It took eighteen months of saving, but by the spring of 1998 he had enough. He went first to the corner by the store to look for a coyote. Nobody was around. He went two doors from his house and spoke to a neighbor, who knew smugglers. Two days later, the neighbor came into the brickyard and told Eduardo it would cost $1,500 to get him to America. With this much money to be made, Eduardo didn't have to look for coyotes. They found him. Just walk with the money and the smugglers will go over mountains and through water to follow you so they can lead.

Eduardo's father had only one thought for him: that liberty is not the country you are in, but the job you have. "If you do not like the job, then you quit and go to another," he said to Eduardo. "It is your only liberty."

People like Silvia and Eduardo had no idea of growing or selling drugs. Crossing the border was about the Job. Because of the drugs, however, they had to face new and imaginative obstacles in order to reach minimum-wage jobs in the United States.

Those carrying drugs into the United States are in the business from the start. A fellow at the New York Botanical Garden gave a lecture one day on the cepas of Bolivia—peasants named after cepa ants, which move as a chain. The human cepas carry packs of coca leaves strapped to their backs from one side of a Bolivian mountain to the crest and then down the hill to the lowlands, where it is cooked into a paste for shipping through Mexico to be sold in the United States, where the demand on Wall Street and in nightclubs and, in rock form, in crack cellars keeps the chain going. Cepas coming down the hill in an unbroken line, one sandal after the other, cepas coming down, cepas going back up the mountain, cepas in a chain draped on a hillside covered with brush. And far off, in Detroit and St. Louis and New York, the stockbrokers hold out cash for powder or, in poor neighborhoods, cash for crack.

Marijuana is smoked so widely in the United States that U.S. law enforcement believes that Mexicans must be wholly responsible. In New York, most pot smokers get their pot by an organized system of messengers, second in size only to the network delivering ad copy and publicity releases and large packages of letters and memos and legal briefs. The papers are carried to offices by bike messengers who are generally black. And then on the streets are these neat white young men pedaling away, carrying knapsacks full of white envelopes. The envelopes are filled with pot and are delivered to offices around Manhattan like take-out food.

The messengers are from offices that take the orders by phone. A woman answers usually, and the caller gives his code: "RF for number 7." As he says this, he can hear the woman typing the number into a computer to verify that the caller is a legitimate customer and not a cop. You get on the list by having a friend call and then the woman gets your name and number and calls you back to make sure you're not the police. After that, you are on the customer list.

Now, ordering pot by phone, you tell the woman what you want. One envelope. They deliver from 2 P.M. to 9 P.M. You have to call before five to get it delivered by nine. They do not deliver heroin or cocaine. That is another and smaller business.

The bicycle messenger is white because cops don't stop whites. He wears a helmet and backpack and carries a driver's license. He brings the envelope up to the reception room of a business, the customer comes out and hands him an envelope with the standard $60, and the messenger gives him the envelope of pot. The guy goes back to his work and the messenger goes out to his bike and wheels his way through heavy Manhattan traffic on his way to the next customer.

Marijuana is so widespread that its status seems to be close to that of booze during Prohibition. You can't actually tell because pot smokers don't talk much. Drinkers boast, "I had a thousand beers last night." Pot smokers are home alone. But the reception rooms have people waiting, and the messengers are in the elevators, and somewhere they are bringing it in across the Mexican border.

OUT OF THE ATTEMPTED sealing of the Mexican border comes a most imaginative and effective drug and illegal immigrant enforcement, and it makes no difference. They find a tunnel of one hundred yards in length between Naco, Sonora, and Naco, Arizona, that has been in use by drug smugglers for twenty years. It was three feet wide and four feet high, and they found about $1.5 million in cash and 2,668 kilos of cocaine. By the time they were through counting the money there was another tunnel.

Stopping illegal immigrants and stopping drug peddlers are two separate and fairly hopeless occupations. In the 280 miles of desert leading to Tucson, authorities intercepted 387,406 people in 1998. The next year, there were 470,449 officially returned Mexicans from this area. The population of Tucson is 460,000. And some people feel a million Mexicans got through, but just enough did not, with 500 dead in the desert, to become an international scandal. Simultaneously, 25 percent of the nation's crime caseload comes from the Mexican border. Federal public defender Sandra Pules sat at her desk one afternoon in early 2000 with case number 3,500. The courtrooms are filled with so many Mexicans, the overwhelming number having to do with illegal crossing. As only one or two guards are available to a courtroom, the Mexicans are always shackled like dangerous animals. All day long, courtrooms are filled with the chiming of chains.

At border crossings like Tijuana and Laredo there are signs up saying that there have been four hundred thousand, five hundred thousand—who knows how many—pounds of pot seized at this location. It is something to be satisfied about, like bridge painting. Upon finishing, you turn and start back, chipping and stroking. With drug arrests and seizures, you catch Mexicans and their drugs; meanwhile the majority of drugs come into the country from Puerto Rico. Drug users are supposedly impoverished and despondent and helplessly addicted, and will steal the nearest silverware. Drug rehabilitation can't possibly be effective with these derelicts. The only thing to do is put a million in prison.

And far away from studies and statistics are the people who use drugs because they are fun. Do I use cocaine? You bet. Am I addicted? Don't be silly. Then why do you use it? I told you. Because it's fun.

The community of Sells, Arizona, sits alone in the border desert on the three-million-acre Tohono O'odham reservation, with its Customs Service patrol. The name Tohono O'odham means "people of the desert." They have been at this place since the sand began. Their ancestors were the Hohokam, who can be traced back to 300 B.C. Agents in this unit must be at least one-quarter Native American.

Here are the two agents from this headquarters pulling up to the three strands of barbed wire that make up the border fortifications. They are Doug Bothof, of the local tribe, and Kevin Carlos, a Sioux from South Dakota. They are here on account of drug smuggling, not illegal aliens. The three strands of wire are the fence that is supposed to be keeping all of Mexico's immigrants and marijuana out. It isn't even government wire. It has been put up by ranchers on the reservation. The top strand has been cut and the end hooked once around the post to hold it up, as if it had not been touched. The second and third strands were the same. Unhook all three and this part of the wire fence becomes a gate.

The two agents watch a van parked just on the other side of the wire, in Mexico. A woman is selling water to the immigrants about to sneak across and whisky to members of the Tohono O'odham tribe who cross over because tribal laws do not allow whisky on their lands.

The agents drive along the wire at five miles an hour, hanging out the windows and training on the ground below the most complex, miraculous technology: eyes that have been trained by their blood since time began to look at the ground and see great pictures and precise diagrams in the empty dirt.

They stop and get out. Bothof looks down at the tire marks of a vehicle that has come right through the wire.

"They're old. You can see people walked across them the next day." The outline of a foot is over that of the tire treads. Then he mutters, "Look at these people. See?" In one spot, a second set of treads suddenly runs over the first set. "They crossed here in two vehicles. Vans, I guess."

"Drugs?" Indicating the footprints.

"Immigrants. The footprints over the treads are too shallow for somebody carrying a heavy pack."

The agents are stocky, with equipment bringing Bothof to about 200 pounds and Carlos up to 260. They carry Steyrs, Austrian rifles with a thirty-round clip, plus another clip on their belts, a radio, receiver, a big Magnum handgun, and a flashlight.

Border areas like this one are speckled with buried sensors that pick up people walking, sometimes even their speech. Any activity lights up on terminals back at the base. But so often the metallic technology isn't worth the air its signals soar through. Whoever passes over the sensor can be gone before anybody gets out to the spot. So the agents track. The depth of the footprints indicates the weight being carried. A person with a backpack of marijuana rubbing, cutting into the shoulders has his feet sinking deeper into the ground than some little illegal carrying only his hopes, who skims across the dust, leaving the imprint of a grasshopper. To desert trackers, the term *backpacker* means a drug carrier, not some Ohio State student on summer break.

Sensors are often made futile by all these centuries of hunting and tracking that run in these border agents. Carlos points out that whether a track is fresh or old can be seen immediately. If the prints of a desert rat are on top of the footprint, it means the footprint is not fresh.

The ones the agents want come across with drugs strapped to their backs. It is usually marijuana, weighing from fifty to seventy-five pounds. The backpackers are usually wrecks who come slogging along until they hit this long stretch of scrub, under a remorseless sky that has them gulping water every few yards. At the start of their trek—back where it was slightly cooler and the paths softer—they can do two miles without stopping. Soon they are down to a mile. Now, outside Sells, they do only a half mile before dropping their packs and collapsing.

They pray to Jesús Malverde, the patron saint of drug peddling: "Let my legs be strong. Let the border guards lose their eyes. Help others know that we carry the good. Nothing that is harmful. Our marijuana causes songs. The Border Patrol kills."

And behind them are the natives with badges, tracking them.

Carlos looks at the bits of branch that have been knocked off bushes by a backpacker lumbering through. He feels the leaves. If they are moist, then somebody just went through. If they're dry, it was a while ago.

The coyotes traveling with the backpackers usually try to cover the track by taking branches and sweeping over the trail, as if they were scrubbing a saloon floor. Always, the sweep marks are a better trail to follow than the footprints.

The coyotes tried tying pieces of carpet to everybody's shoes, causing a smoothness where there was supposed to be footprints. Noticing this, the trackers began to sift the dirt. They found colored fabric strands from the carpet. They followed them. Next, the drug packers used mop rope, with strands the color of sand, but it still showed fresh and bright in the agents' eyes.

The drug haulers left signs where they sat to rest. One time, there were traces leading up to the start of mountains, and then on the rocks they found a small boulder dislodged, another overturned when somebody slipped and kicked it. Soon the agents were on four backpackers sitting with five huge packs of marijuana. Bothof was waiting for them to say they didn't know anything about the extra pack. Instead, one of them said it belonged to a group that was just over the next small slope. Which they were. On that day, there were thirteen arrests, and hundreds of pounds of marijuana were confiscated.

Over the course of a year the unit seizes 640,000 pounds of drugs. They are tremendous. They stop a third of what comes across. Because of his ability, Kevin Bothof was sent to Uzbekistan and Kazakhstan to show the police of these states, once part of the Soviet Union, how to track people trying to smuggle nuclear weapons to terrorists in places like Pakistan. When Bothof arrived, the police thought he was going to have sophisticated technology to show them. Instead he said he worked only with a stick and a knife and a lot of walking and bending. Any day now, his expertise will have him back in Uzbekistan.

Yet with all the history and energy, you still have as much chance of stopping drugs as you do of swimming to China. An hour and a half's drive away, in the Mexican town of Nuevo Nogales, there was a dispute over a dispute, and somebody walked across the street to the border crossing station and announced that there were two bastards coming across in their pickup truck with cocaine. By the time the word was passed along, the two Mexicans were through the desert and into Arizona, driving on Highway 19 in their 1997 Ford Lobo double-cab pickup, the truck's windshield smacked up and its rear license plate hammered around, but not enough to obscure its numbers, which had been reported by the stool pigeon. Here was a lone police officer who had just been advised to be on the lookout for a pickup with two men and a lot of cocaine. The policeman needed no surveillance system shooting data to a satellite near the moon and then back to his machine on earth to identify the pickup. Nor did he need a copy of the Constitution to know that he had a right to stop the vehicle; every car is a violation, even parked in the garage—a certificate is pasted in the wrong part of the window, the license plate isn't attached properly. This vehicle also had over six hundred pounds of cocaine. So a common patrolman with a panting German shepherd in the back pulled the pickup over. The Nogales police had received a phone call about the truck. All the cop had to do was look and press the button for his siren to make them stop.

The cop came out of the car with the dog. The police said that upon sniffing at the pickup, the dog went insane.

"*Él huele el sandwich,*" one of the Mexicans said. He smells the sandwich.

He could have been right. No matter how well bred, how strictly trained, a dog's sniff is for fresh liverwurst. Plus, a handler and his dog must be together for some time if they are going to be effective. Smelling is a two-man game. But often you'll have the handler transferred and a new one taking over, and by the time this one and the dog are familiar with each other, the officer is up for a new post, and the next guy not only is new but hates dogs. That means the police dog isn't worth the leash he comes on.

This time, who knows what the dog on the highway outside of

Nogales smelled? That didn't matter because the cop knew that there was cocaine on the truck. There sure was. He tugged and pulled out 607 pounds of cocaine. The two Mexicans in the truck shrugged. They didn't know what the cop was talking about.

Usually, figures that police announce as to the value of seized narcotics are fantasy. This time anybody with experience could tell you that in New York you certainly could get $6 million for the packages.

And it was discovered by a local phone call, which is the technology used in the ancient method of informing, not with any skilled trackers. Which is a sign of the hopelessness of fighting drugs. For if one truck with 607 pounds is found this way, you need no imagination to estimate all the organized smuggling that doesn't get stopped. Maybe they stopped half a mountainside of cocaine, which was worth millions and millions in a big city. The trouble was, the other half of the mountain came through the border in another pickup truck. Lawmen on the border learned of this some days later.

On the highways around Nogales, I-92 and I-80, right in the middle of the barren land, suddenly there is a traffic tie-up that seems like the entrance to the Lincoln Tunnel in New York. There are cars and trucks sitting on the highway, and finally up ahead are the flashing red lights of law enforcement. The traffic moves slowly. Now traffic cones push the cars and trucks into one lane. There is a small military green tank trailer, which holds water. There are white Border Patrol vans parked, a large van, and a table with agents around it. Out on the road are many Border Patrol agents. One pokes into a car or truck for a few moments, the vehicles move out of the one lane and onto the highway, and he looks into the next in line. Now you are even with the Border Patrol people. Sunglasses, trim mustache, great big gun on his belt, he looks in. No warrant, no discussion. He just looks in. Then he pulls his head out. "Have a nice day." The hand waves and you drive off.

Twenty minutes later, the traffic is backed up again. A van full of Mexicans is being held on the side of the road. The dog and his handler walk around the van and get nowhere.

But there are Mexicans out on the roadside. The big trucks with white drivers go right on through.

"Good afternoon, folks," the Border Patrol guy says as the next car pulls up.

He starts to put his head in.

"You got a warrant?" he is asked.

"We're within twenty-five miles of the border and we have the right to search," he says.

Now his head comes in, he sees the three whites in the car, and his head comes out.

"Have a good day."

Mexicans come into Nogales like blowing sand. And every step is dedicated to silence. This is a town where the most prominent sound in the still air is made by the warning bells of the railroad crossing gates on the freight tracks that run through the center of the town. When the striped gate arms go down, the cars and a small crowd of mostly women with paper shopping bags wait on the street. Three diesel locomotives hooked to each other—two Southern Pacific and a Union Pacific, with all engines throbbing— run through the crossing. Their red and green sides glare in the sun even through the coating of grime. The engineers sit high over the street with chins resting on arms. In a town of adventurers, they pose as the most exciting. The engines go through the crossing and run down the tracks behind buildings and stop. The bells commence and the crossing gates go up. The drivers cross the tracks, the women shoppers rush to the other side. A whistle sounds from one of the engines. The bells chime and the gates come down, halting traffic. The engines back up through the crossing and run on up the tracks a couple of hundred yards to freight cars with several workmen waiting. The crossing gates remain down as the freight cars are coupled to the locomotives. With a whistle, the locomotives come back to the crossing, pulling their freight cars. Suddenly they stop at the crossing. The engineers stare down. The gates are down and the locals sit frustrated in their cars. Finally the locomotives pull the freight cars out of the way and disappear down the tracks. Citizens of Nogales complain that the engines block the crossing out of insolence, to show the majesty of the rails. This controversy spills over to the local newspaper, whose stories are picked up by Tucson television. This was the major local news in a town that everywhere else, from movies to nightly news, was the stage for the cops and robbers of the international drug trade. It also was the place where the wave of immigrants drew itself up and then cascaded across the sand and into America.

Despite the large numbers of immigrants who came in without danger, for many the crossing turned into torture. So many Mexicans, afraid of the Border Patrol at Nogales, circle into the desert to find their way across the border. Others risk arrest and simply jump a border fence or crawl through sewers.

The business street in Nogales ends at a new coffee shop that is owned by a young woman whose husband is with the Nogales police department. She says that she gets a good trade of police as they come off duty.

A few yards down from the coffee shop, there is the high sheet-metal fence and a border crossing point, a tiny customs station with two passageways. On the left as you walk up, a customs agent sits on a straight-back chair and makes sure that the Mexicans who came through have their border identification passes. The people taking the other short passageway, to Nuevo Nogales, need to show nothing. They take a few steps through the passageway and come out into the riot of the first street of Nuevo Nogales. On one corner is a crowd of men, cab drivers, hangers-on, who gave the appearances of being open to any proposition. On the opposite corner is an old building with a big Times Square sign: Girls! Girls! Girls! Underneath it is the less flamboyant and more comforting Liquor.

From the border crossing station, the fence runs up a hill that immediately becomes steep. At the top there is a house on the Mexican side that is right up against the fence. The front porch of the house is as high as the fence and requires only the easiest of leaps to go from the porch to America.

"Where does the fence end?" the customs agent was asked.

"Right up there a few hundred yards out of town."

"What happens when the fence ends?"

"They all come through," he said, waving a hand. Yet too few realize this and go out into a dangerous desert.

At the top of a hot dirt hill, whose street signs said East East Street, there was a Postal Service jeep parked on the side street, North Short Street. It was a low-level slum of houses that appeared to be empty. The street ended at the border fence a few yards away. On the other side of the fence, at the house with the porch touching the fence, a man stood and watched the mailman, Tom McAlpin. Tom was born in Cabrini Hospital on the East Side of Manhattan and has a distant connection to the old Hotel McAlpin on Thirty-fourth Street. He was opening rows of silver mailboxes on a neighborhood stand outside one of the dry, cracked one-story houses. He said that there were no mixups with letters to Nuevo Nogales, Mexico, and to Nogales, Arizona, because, he said proudly, they handle the mail with great efficiency at the post office.

"The Border Patrol parks here a half hour, then goes off for a half hour, then comes back, but they still come over the fence as if nobody was around," McAlpin said. "They put a baby in a basket and lower him over the fence on a rope. Then the father climbs over the fence after him. Sometimes they ask if they can hand me the baby while they climb over. I'm not against the kid. I was a baby myself. But the least I can do for my country is not help them break the law. Besides, we had some guy take the baby and the Mexican jumped over holding another kid and he breaks his leg. The Mexican with the broken leg gets taken to the hospital and who knows when you see him again. Now the guy here has not only one baby but two."

"Where do they go when they don't break their legs?"

He looked around the street of silent decrepit houses, the fronts overgrown. "The house right behind us. I don't want to look, but you can. Just quick."

The house was boarded up and had a rusted tin roof.

"I bet there's thirty-five of them in there now," he said. "They call this a safe house. Sleep on the floor with rats. Then they get out of here. They go up to Terrace Avenue and catch a van."

On Terrace Avenue, there are two hundred licensed taxis and parking lots filled with vans with signs advertising Nogales-Tucson or Nogales-Phoenix. The taxis are numerous, but they, along with cars, can be confiscated if the Border Patrol finds the back packed with Mexicans. The law states that vans cannot be grabbed no matter how many passengers are yanked out and taken to the detention center. Of course the Greyhound buses are best. Nobody touches them.

The vans are for rushing immigrants away from Nogales and on the way to their American dream. One woman van driver complained to the mailman that it was a slow day. "She says she's made only thirteen hundred dollars so far today," he said.

At 42 Terrace Avenue, five men sit under an umbrella in front of a store. None of them has a job, and all of them are on cell phones. They look over a rail at the thousands of cars coming through the customs plaza from Mexico. They know what they are looking for in the river of metal. A fortune coming through in one car, two cars, three cars, maybe a dozen cars.

The largest number of immigrants coming through Nogales—when overwhelmed, the county sheriff says a million a year, and thus far nobody has refuted him—come by foot. All the sophisticated sensors and night lighting and cameras are in the end useless against a population that starts moving like a glacier. In Nogales the modern technology comes down to two Border Patrol vans parked on the highway going out of town and looking into the mouth of the town's sewer drain. The moment they are not there, out of the sewer, scrambling like crabs, come waves of people from Nuevo Nogales. They spread across the land and head north, crossing the ranches of people like Sara Ann Bailey, who at sixty-eight sits on a tractor somewhere on her five-hundred-acre ranch with a .380 Smith and Wesson pistol in her jeans. She bought it at Wal-Mart for $150. She also has a sawed-off Mosberg shotgun at her feet. She grows hybrid grass, sudan-sorghum, on seventy irrigated acres for cattle grazing and is out there from 8 A.M. to 4 P.M. every day, driving the tractor alone through acres of bushes and low trees. Sometimes an illegal immigrant suddenly appears a few yards away. She has never shot at a Mexican, nor has anybody on the surrounding ranches. She served as a federal magistrate in Nogales for five years and never heard of a Mexican carrying anything but a knife or club to protect himself from snakes or the four-legged coyotes or an occasional sixty-pound mountain lion. Yet the immigrants scare her. When the Mexicans see that she is armed, they disappear in the brush. She lives her days like this. In 1982, an immigrant named Martínez Villareal broke into her house twice. First he stole art, which he sold at the train station in Nogales, Sonora. Then he stole two hunting rifles. He went to the next ranch and had a run-in with the foreman and a cowboy and he shot them dead with one of her rifles. He is still on death row, and she has never gotten over it.

She lives alone in the ranch house with three dogs inside, three outside in a large run, and three roaming loose. She has sensors in the ground around the house, a siren on the roof, and burglar alarms on the doors and windows. One night, a couple of hundred immigrants came across her property. She had her mother, age ninety-six, with her, and the Mexicans began tapping on her window to see if anybody was home. The woman could no longer take it. She let the dogs loose. And she gave return taps on the window with the barrel of her Mosberg shotgun. While the increases in the Border Patrol have cut the number of people roaming across her grounds to only a dozen or so a night, Sara Ann Bailey still has her shotgun for window duty.

The smoke and sand of the border carries with it something much more dangerous than leaves that make people dizzy and dazed. Over in Texas, almost to San Antonio, there is a Border Patrol stop, but it is just another obstacle to brush past.

At Dixon, Illinois, a trailer truck was stopped on the highway and state police were inspecting it for violations, they said, but they were really going over it for drugs.

In New York, a police commissioner named Howard Safir, who came out of a third-rate drug enforcement agency to pander his way into the New York job, attended several conferences in Washington in which Border Patrol people described their tremendous success in stopping drug peddlers. They gave reasons for search and seizure that would not play in New York, even if the police chief was all for it and his mayor, as sick as they come, would love it. A judge would thwart them. So on the East Side of Manhattan at Thirty-sixth Street, a block short of the entrance to the Queens-Midtown Tunnel, the police had traffic cones set up and cars had to roll slowly through a wall of police. A cop stops you.

"Hi. This a friendly stop," he says.

"Have you got a warrant?" he is asked.

"I said it's a friendly stop." He hands in a flyer. "You can go up to the yard on the West Side and get a free car inspection," he said. "It'll be good for your insurance."

The flyer gave directions to the lot where the police keep towed vehicles. Of course they would look over your car for drugs.

They couldn't do it here on the street without a warrant. But if you took the car to the pound, then they could go over it for the least smattering of drugs, top to tires. A catastrophe blots out the Constitution. Streets are closed, pedestrians stopped, and police play martial law by blocking traffic for hours.

The stop is more proof that each puff of powdered dirt coming from Mexican footsteps far away at the border is a smoke signal that you can lose your liberty as it always is lost, a yard at a time, a mile at a time, a stop at a time.

CHAPTER TEN

After being dumped back into Mexico, Silvia, her uncle Rogelio, and her friend Moisés went back to the Fontana Hotel, and all three made small moans when they had to pay another $400 for the room. Silvia bought a phone card at a stand next door, after which she called her cousin Belén in College Station.

"You know what? They sent me back," Silvia remembers calling out over the phone.

The cousin told her, "You'll do it again. Everybody who tries again makes it."

The cousin gave her the name of a coyote who was known for getting people through quicker than the ones Silvia had used. "If you need money, I can give you some," the cousin said.

Silvia, Rogelio, and Moisés went to a small restaurant on the same street as the hotel. Silvia asked the cashier if the coyote her cousin recommended was known. The cashier said sure. Silvia gave the cashier the hotel room number.

They sat down to have tortilla sandwiches.

"I can't wait to cross again," Silvia said.

Moisés lowered his eyes and ate his sandwich. The uncle arched his brows in a questioning look. Silvia remembers telling herself, the two of them want to go home.

"You don't want to go to Texas?" she said to Moisés.

"Why is it better than San Matías?" he said.

"Maybe it isn't," said Rogelio.

"You can make more money in Texas," she said.

"I don't like the river," he told her.

He didn't. He had turned many colors of fear when the cold water came up to his chin on the river crossing.

"Did the river frighten you?" she said to her uncle.

"No, it did not frighten me. It was just that it was cold."

She remembered the same cold as he did, but didn't bring it up. When they came back to the hotel, a burly guy with a wood match in his mouth talked to them. Yes, he remembered Silvia's cousin. He got her to Texas, and she paid. He could trust them and they could trust him. He needed $1,200 from each to get across the border.

The uncle swallowed. He had borrowed money from everyone in the family to get the original $600. Moisés winced. He even had some of Eduardo's money in his pocket. They went up to the room to talk it over. It was late afternoon. Silvia stretched out on the bed. Moisés was on the floor. Her uncle Rogelio sat in a chair and looked at her.

They talked for a half hour, during which she discovered that they had two choices in mind: either get the night bus to Puebla and San Matías, or wait until the morning bus. Silvia told Moisés that she knew Eduardo would try again if he were here, and therefore he should honor Eduardo's loan and try again. Moisés shrugged. She told her uncle that she would not dare call home to tell the family that she couldn't go because her uncle wanted to come home. She told Moisés that her father had told her that the only way he would let her go was with the uncle. If she called him now, he would make her come home. Her uncle said nothing.

Now, after thirty minutes of getting nowhere, Silvia put a slight tremor in her voice and a small sadness in her eyes. She said that she was going to continue. As she had no brothers to protect her, she only had Rogelio, the uncle, and Moisés, the friend. When she had left San Matías with them, she felt like they were her real brothers. She had counted on them and still did. Don't let me go across the border alone, she said. I am afraid. Tears in her eyes. She was still fifteen years old.

This time they were taken on a different path to the river, which was knee deep with a lazy current at the point they crossed.

As they were paying $1,200 each, they were driven in a Honda Accord to a house in the center of nowhere. Silvia's cousin had wired money by Western Union to the coyote at the Fontana. They were the hardest dollars in the land. After a couple of years of work, she was empty. But she was expected to put up the money. Mexican families are large, with cousins usually taking the role of friends. When somebody needs money, especially to get to America, the family pitches in. There she was, an expensive traveler at fifteen and a half years old, but she was sure she would be able to repay the cousin quickly because of the good paying job she was sure to get.

Now, the coyote, with payment for a second trip in his pocket, moved Silvia's party from the house into an auto repair shop next door. Her uncle and Moisés stretched out on the greasy floor. Silvia was awarded an old couch that was about as busted down and filthy as you can get, but she remembers that it felt luxurious. The coyote took a look at the uncle and Silvia in the morning. The men's clothes looked like they had been clawed by a mountain lion. Silvia's clothes were also shredded. The coyote said they could not land in the Houston airport dressed like that. They would be arrested and their plane impounded. He disappeared and returned with new jeans and shirts.

After that, they drove to a private airstrip. A man put five of

them into a single-engine plane and flew them to Houston. Silvia
and her uncle and Moisés got into a cab and said they wanted to
go to College Station. The cab driver said he wanted to see their
papers. Silvia's uncle showed him money. Two hours later, she
walked into the bare rooms of a ground-floor apartment in College
Station, Texas. There was only a table and a couple of chairs, and
bedding on the floor inside the two rooms where they would sleep.
Silvia would start out by sleeping in one of the crowded rooms. But
only for now. A tape player was on the living room floor. Silvia took
a cassette out of her suitcase and put it on. The soft music of Bryndis filled the barren room.

SILVIA GOT UP on the first morning and went up the block to an
Olive Garden restaurant. They hired her as kitchen help. The hours
were 4 P.M. to midnight.

　　Several blocks from there was a barbecue restaurant. She got a
job making salads from seven A.M. until noon.

　　She was fifteen and a half years old and she was in America
and she was working sixty-five hours a week and she thought it was
glorious. She was earning $420 a week, the salary of a rich person
in Mexico. When he hears how much I am making, Eduardo will
come to College Station, she told herself.

CHAPTER ELEVEN

Eduardo's mother didn't like the idea of her son leaving. She had a vision of a place she had never seen, of dark buildings rising from a black volcano. She pointed to the black smoke covering the snow at the top of the simmering volcano that rose out of the struggling land outside Puebla. It was many miles away, but still too close for her. "Something will happen," she told Eduardo. "New York is too big."

The father remembers blessing him at the airport, which was the only show of emotion between them. Eduardo flew to Tijuana.

When Eduardo got off the plane, a young guy wearing a black shirt met him, and Eduardo followed him to a taxi. He asked if they were going to the blue pharmacy that Chockaloo had glorified. The coyote smirked. The pharmacy, he said, faced an army camp. They rode for twenty minutes to an old sprawling ranch house that sat in the dust and scrub. Inside the house was a series of cubicles with twenty-five young Mexicans sleeping on the floor. The place had been set up as a motel, Eduardo thought, but they probably saw it was far better to fill it with Mexicans paying some of their $1,500 here, rather than running a motel renting for $49 a day to people in love. Eduardo gave the coyote $1,000 of the payment due. He'd hand over the remainder when he reached New York. This was a pleasant fiction, as if he could withhold payment somehow. Both he and the coyote knew that he could be killed for $500. The coyotes were smuggling people because they didn't want to risk decades in jail for drug smuggling. A drug smuggler would spit at $500; the immigrant smuggler would kill for it.

Eduardo waited there for eight days. For food, he walked down to a Taco Bell, which stood on the edge of town. He was in Mexico, but if anybody made him for what he was, a young guy with money in his pocket to pay a coyote, they would become so jealous that they would not be able to restrain themselves from going out with a shotgun and robbing him, or rushing to the police to report the presence of somebody about to commit an illegal act by crossing the border. The Mexican border police had a reputation of snatching anybody they thought was going over the border, issuing a beating, and taking the person's money.

Ted Conover wrote in his book *Coyotes* that he and a Mexican were stopped by Mexican judicial police. They took the Mexican into a room, tilted his head back, covered his mouth, and poured carbonated water up his nose and into the sinuses. The Mexican screamed to God during the torture. Then they took his money.

Eduardo waited for eight days, while the twenty-five Mexicans in the ranch house increased to over fifty. Sleeping was accomplished with somebody's foot in the face.

At $1,500 a head, the cash value of this group was somewhere close to $75,000. The money had to be split among the local steerers back in the Mexican towns, the coyotes on duty at the Mexican border, the owners of the safe houses on both sides of the border, and the drivers, who considered their trips hazardous and demanded real money. They also had to buy airline tickets for those being smuggled all the way to New York. At the end, the money had to be like anything else in crime, something for boasting but not buying, because despite the news reports of $200,000 Bentleys, you can't hand a car dealer a pocketful of dust.

Finally, a truck pulled up outside and a fat man with plaid pants and a black shirt got out, and Eduardo's friend Mariano remembers hearing him call to Eduardo and those around him, "All right. Let's go. Get up. We're going to start walking."

They remember walking for two hours through scrub and up into the first high hills that ran into gloomy mountains that climbed above the highway. The fat man led them to a black van that sat in the bushes. They got into the van, elbows into each other, and the fat man drove them the five hours to Phoenix. In a deserted block of low factories closed for the weekend, they pulled up alongside another van. Eduardo and the others had no idea of whether they were in Mexico or the United States. This time, they were driven all the way back to Los Angeles. The fat man explained that this was the most direct route to Los Angeles from Tijuana. These coyotes were knowledgeable about getting through the desert and rivers to America, perhaps, but they seemed cockeyed whenever they read a map of America. At the Los Angeles airport, the fat driver waved to a guy lounging at the baggage desk in front of the American Airlines section. The young guy walked up and handed Eduardo a ticket to New York.

At Kennedy Airport, Eduardo remembered going up to the New York coyote who awaited him. He started to give the guy the remaining $500, knowing he would be shot dead if he tried to leave the airport without paying. The coyote stopped him, saying it would look like a narcotics transaction. They walked outside the terminal and down to the end of the walkway, where Eduardo handed him the cash. Somebody would come to take him on the subway to Brighton Beach, which is in Brooklyn, in America.

Once, they came in dreadful old ships, from Magilligan in Northern Ireland, from Cobh in southern Ireland, from Liverpool and Naples and Palermo and Odessa. The prow went into gray

waves with freezing white foam whipping from them, and sometimes it seemed that the prow would not come up and that it would
take the whole ship under the gray water. When it finally came up,
the passengers vomited and fell off bunks and cried; an old man
died and a woman was unconscious and babies bled. Those able to
stand always scoured the horizon, through sleet and snow swirls, for
the first look at the city where the streets were decorated, if not
paved, with gold.

But this was the spring of 1998, and Eduardo was entering a
town whose mayor was Rudolph Giuliani. He would get lucky with
a war and become an improbable hero. But now he was merely a
strange, sneering man who attracted people equally strange, particularly a chief of staff, Bruce Teitelbaum. Teitelbaum was Jewish and
a Republican, and in New York this is as common as a camel train.

Eduardo had never heard of either of them, and Giuliani had
nothing to do with him, but unfortunately Teitelbaum did. Teitelbaum covered the distance from City Hall to Williamsburg and was
the connection, the pull, the clout, in the city administration. He
was the major fund-raiser for Giuliani in the Hasidic communities.
The position of fund-raiser is one of the few with power in a government. The word *power* is almost always misused, for most
municipal gnomes have none, except in the case of Teitelbaum, who
took over something called the Vacancy Control Board. This is a
one-man group hidden from view in the basement of City Hall; it
decides who can work in city government, who can be transferred,
and who can be pushed out of work. Nobody knows what the
Vacancy Control Board is except for those begging for a job and
pledging to break any rule, tell any lie, bury any report.

Simultaneously, there were no rules for a builder, particularly in
Hasidic neighborhoods, other than putting up money on demand
for politicians.

Politicians recall first noticing Teitelbaum at a Giuliani rally in the Hasidic Borough Park section of Brooklyn. He didn't understand what he was doing, but he acted as if he did. Which immediately irritated Dov Hikind, the state legislator who ran the rally. It created an atmosphere of intense dislike that later caused Hikind, on trial in federal court for the totally false charge of stealing, to claim that Teitelbaum had put him there. Hikind went on to say that the day was soon coming when Teitelbaum would cry on the way to prison. This deepest dislike shot up from the platform at that first outdoor rally. It was the usual and understandable procedure for a campaign. In all of them, people hand out leaflets and rumors; many of the faces are crossed with insanity. In this case, the venom lasted beyond normal loathing.

Bruce Teitelbaum turned into a city figure when he rose out of a seat at Lincoln Center, where he sat with Mayor Giuliani at a concert of the New York Philharmonic in honor of the United Nations leaders. In the great hall was the Palestine Liberation Organization's Yasir Arafat, who had received tickets from the United Nations. Immediately, the flames shot ceilingward from Mayor Giuliani and his aide, Teitelbaum. How could this murderer be allowed at your concert? Teitelbaum asked Giuliani. Yes, Giuliani said, I don't run concerts for killers. Get him out of here.

Teitelbaum got up and walked over to Arafat and his two aides. It was during the second movement of Beethoven's Ninth Symphony. Teitelbaum told Arafat and his aides that they had to leave. The mayor didn't want them.

He told this to Arafat and his people while looking to the left and then the right and then up above. At least a few nearby noticed that Teitelbaum displayed such nervousness that it appeared he would collapse. Arafat sat there for a few moments. One of his aides said they had thought about staying because of the mantle of the UN, which was what Giuliani expected. That he had embarrassed them would be sufficient. Then he could say Arafat stayed because of the anti-Israeli UN. But Arafat decided to let them drown in acid. He and his aides stood and walked out in the middle of the performance.

Bruce Teitelbaum, high apprehension subsided, now swaggered like a wild boar. He was indisputably the most important Jewish name in city affairs. He was next to a mayor who did virtually nothing each day except to get into the papers or to meet girlfriends. He was content to have Teitelbaum keep the people in love with him, and if it meant Teitelbaum giving contracts out to Jewish organizations, then let him do all he wants of it. Giuliani was going to run for president or vice president or senator, whatever, and it would cost tens of millions, and Teitelbaum knew how to get the money.

Much of it came from builders, who are crooks with blueprints and are thus at ease with people in City Hall. Teitelbaum handled anything that was needed to keep someone like Eugene Ostreicher, the father, sending in the cash. Joseph Spitzer, who lives in a building on Fifty-ninth Street in Brooklyn's Borough Park along with Richie Ostreicher, the son, is celebrated for bringing $83,000 into Giuliani campaigns. Nothing in New York—no fire chief complaining, and certainly no young Mexican—is allowed to get in the way of that. "How could you say that we gave him the city for his eighty-three thousand?" Teitelbaum said. "We raised eight hundred and thirty thousand dollars from builders. Spitzer gave eighty-three thousand." Spitzer was given a placard that allowed him to park almost anywhere in the city. He usually could be found in the City Hall offices of Teitelbaum and then his successor as the chief of staff of the Giuliani office, Anthony Carbonetti. Whatever Spitzer needed done, they did.

AT FIRST, THIS SEEMS to start in another universe from an obstacle to building in Williamsburg that required help from City Hall. In the 1930s, Louis Carbonetti and Harold Giuliani, the mayor's father, grew up together in East Harlem, on the streets of Tommy (Three-

Finger Brown) Lucchese, Joey Rao, and Trigger Mike Coppola. Harold Giuliani pulled burglaries and holdups. He told the court he did it because of unemployment. He went to Sing Sing prison for sixteen months. Carbonetti did not go to prison. Louis Carbonetti became a second for professional fighters, a bucket carrier who between rounds would lean over the ropes and clean a fighter's cuts. While Carbonetti attended school on First Avenue and in Stillman's Gymnasium on Eighth Avenue, he received a merit appointment as assistant secretary to a new state supreme court judge, Thomas Aurelio. Carbonetti's merit was that he knew Aurelio, and also every mob guy in his district. A wiretap of Frank Costello, prime minister of the underworld, and Aurelio was played in public by authorities hoping to block Aurelio. On it, Aurelio said, "Francesco, how can I thank you?" And Costello said, "When I tell you it's in the bag, it's done."

When he came out of prison, Harold Giuliani married a young neighborhood woman and moved to Brooklyn, where he worked saloons, collecting for bookmakers and loan sharks. His son, Rudy, was born in Brooklyn. Harold took his son to East Harlem on Sundays, where they saw neighborhood friends and then went with the father's friend, Lou Carbonetti, to games at Yankee Stadium. Harold Giuliani then moved Rudy to the Long Island suburbs, taking him away from street life.

Carbonetti wound up being defeated for a Democratic district leadership in East Harlem. That left him jobless; you can't be in a judge's office if you lose your own district. But he had his own cut man, East Harlem's city councilman, the Rev. Louis Gigante. His brother, Vincent (The Chin) Gigante, ran the underworld, but he never as much as served mass for his brother. Father Gigante was to become a true builder of his city, as opposed to a cheap talentless developer. At the most searing, disturbing time in the Bronx, when fires and hopelessness were beyond anybody's capacity to repel, Governor Nelson Rockefeller sent his housing administrator, Edward

Logue, to visit Gigante at his parish, St. Athanasius. "Is there some way you could build up here, or are the threats and violence too much?" he asked Gigante.

"We do not tolerate violence. We do not accept threats," Gigante said.

With state subsidies, Gigante took empty buildings and turned them into new apartments. Over three thousand people lined up for a day and a half to apply for his first apartments.

"God bless Father Gigante forever," Logue announced.

Logue then wrote a famous memo to Rockefeller: "Suppliers and sub-contractors and vandals tend to hesitate before bothering Father Gigante."

Father Lou often could be found in the 115th Street clubhouse of Anthony (Fat Tony) Salerno, who was the second in charge of Vincent Gigante's gang. Tony was the Tip O'Neill of the underworld and would reside forever in Rudy Giuliani's mind. Rudy had to know Tony from early years just by walking the street with his father and Carbonetti. Fat Tony was twelve when he drove a truck for Dutch Schultz. Later, Fat Tony's club, the Palma Boy Club—there is no *s* because there is no *s*—on 115th was around the corner from Lou Carbonetti's Democratic district clubhouse.

The man from around the corner from Fat Tony's old head-quarters, Louis Carbonetti, now became the first Carbonetti to work in City Hall. When Abe Beame was the mayor and Father Gigante's friend, and Stanley Friedman was his chief assistant, Father Gigante took Carbonetti down to City Hall and as much as put him in an office and said, "Here's where you work."

He had a son, Lou Carbonetti Jr., who would be the first to follow him onto the city payroll.

Rudy Giuliani went on to become the United States attorney for New York. He made sure he became famous as the zealot who broke the Mafia. Familiarity. At the same time he had a fascination with mafiosi and even imitated Fat Tony Salerno's speech. A Giuliani indictment brought Fat Tony into federal court in a trial of Mafia bosses. Giuliani did not prosecute Fat Tony himself, but it was his indictment. At a break one day, Fat Tony got up and brushed past guards who were supposed to stop him and went to the railing in front of the spectators' rows. A man waiting at the rail handed Fat Tony a cigar. Fat Tony inspected it. The day before, when the same man had brought Fat Tony a cigar, the mobster had exclaimed, "Bring me a thing like this!" and broke the cigar in half and threw it on the floor. This time, the man said, "It's Cuban, Tony."

Salerno grunted and put the cigar in the breast pocket of his suit.

Now he said, loudly enough for the large room to hear, "Did you bring me a gun?" He pointed at the prosecutor. "I want to shoot this prick."

Then he motioned to the judge. "I'd like to fuckin' shoot her, too."

Later in the trial, they played a wiretap of Mafia capital punishment jury deliberations. Fat Tony put on a large yellow headset to listen. It also could be heard on speakers in the courtroom. The tape played for about a half hour, and every voice in crime except Fat Tony's was on it voting to have someone killed. In the spectators' front row, Fat Tony's man brightened. He gave a satisfied nod to Fat Tony. Listening through the earphones in the front of the room, Fat Tony made a face that said, all right.

At this moment there came over the tape the one decisive vote of the mob. It was the unmistakable voice of Fat Tony Salerno calling out, "Hit!"

Fat Tony shrugged. What are you going to do? "Good night, Irene," he muttered to the guys at the defense table,

The Carbonettis—father, son, and eventually grandson and wife—worked in the two mayoral campaigns of Harold Giuliani's son, Rudy. When Giuliani won, he had Lou Carbonetti Jr. helping to hand out city patronage jobs. Then Lou junior had a private copying business that folded and he owed $100,000. It was discovered that he used two driver's licenses. He had to leave the regular city government and take over a private neighborhood organization called a Business Improvement District. His former wife, JoAnna Aniello, received a job in city housing.

The grandson, Anthony Carbonetti, was made the patronage dispenser for the city, under Bruce Teitelbaum. He then was made the chief of staff of the whole administration. Carbonetti's resumé is nonexistent. His last job before City Hall was that of a bartender in Boston. On his 1994 financial disclosure forms he listed a scorching hand at Atlantic City as a source of income.

By 1998, he didn't need slot machines. His salary at City Hall was $115,000. Public jobs are never supposed to give the appearance of impropriety. While gambling in Atlantic City is legal, and you're even entitled to report winnings no matter how preposterous the claim, for somebody in New York's City Hall, it still looks at least lousy.

Carbonetti and the English language were opponents. Some of the most painful moments in City Hall came whenever he sat in his small office and dictated letters. Incidentally, the size and location of a government office is meaningless. Bare and shabby are common. It is the phone or the memo that does it.

Anthony Carbonetti also was as subtle as a thrown brick. On the phone, he told commissioners, "You've got to do this. Just do it. Don't ask me anything. Just do it. This is for a friend of the mayor's." His special interest was the Brooklyn Hasidic community. He didn't have to bother with calls and return calls with Hasidim. Sitting in his office was Joseph Spitzer, who owns a huge four-story house in Borough Park. It has a marble front and a stoop with polished brass banisters. Records show that residents of this house included Chaim Ostreicher, Eugene's son, and Faye Schwimmer, Ostreicher's daughter and Leon Schwimmer's daughter-in-law. It was helpful to find this on record, for Ostreicher and those around him denied the fact that the house even existed. "We don't know Spitzer," one yelled. "He has zero to do with us."

Spitzer talked to Carbonetti, and Carbonetti talked to a commissioner.

If you had building violations or even a building collapse and were Hasidic, City Hall took care of everything. What did a report by a building inspector or a fireman mean? The builder was the mayor's friend, or had relatives raising funds for him.

A Mexican immigrant like Eduardo Daniel Gutiérrez didn't count.

CHAPTER TWELVE

Eduardo moved into a space on an upstairs floor in an attached frame house that was across the street from Grady High School in Brighton Beach. The landlord, who lived on the first floor, was never seen, and the Mexicans were crowded onto the second. There was a kitchen, bathroom, a small bedroom, and a large front bedroom with dark brown paneling and a blue carpet. The large bedroom had two windows looking down at the stoop and street. A television set was in one corner of the room. Eight from Mexico slept and lived there when Eduardo arrived. They slept on the floor on thin pads and pillows. You picked your place to sleep and then it became yours. Eduardo slept between Alejandro and Mariano Ramirez, Gustavo's brother. They had their heads to the wall under the windows. The room was long enough so that their feet did not touch those of the others sleeping with their heads against the opposite wall.

Eduardo was stunned by the bathroom. Never before had he seen one in a house. With nine people and one bathroom, there was an implied agreement that each would take no more than ten minutes. He soon learned that each time somebody slipped past

him, it would be ten minutes of listening to running water. Let three
get ahead and you lose a half hour. He realized that he had to
stand around as if thinking of something and then suddenly jump at
first click of the bathroom door opening. He often lost out to a
shoulder and a fully slammed door. The most familiar sound in the
house was that of someone rapping on the bathroom door to get
the occupant to hurry.

In the kitchen there was a stove and a sink; a house with running water in San Matías was at best rare. A turn of the handle
brought a flame out of the stovetop. Magic. There was a large
round table for the group to eat at. They each paid $95 a month in
rent and $25 a week for food. Martha, who was the sister of Gus-
tavo and Mariano, lived in the small bedroom with her husband.
She was on the lease and handled the rents and cooking. Martha
had three children at home in San Matías with her mother in the
rooms right behind where Eduardo's family lived. Her brother Gustavo had left two children in Mexico with his wife. One day Gustavo's wife left the children with Gustavo's mother in San Matías
and said she was going to look for work. Instead, she went off with
a man and never returned. This left the grandmother in San Matías
with six grandchildren. All her upbringing and beliefs told her there
was something worse ahead, a catastrophe, a tragedy falling from
the sky, and she never could see it, but now suddenly it was in front
of her at night. In a dream she had, she was in line at the window of
the appliance store for the money order from Brighton Beach in
Brooklyn, and instead of a man with her money order, there was a
skull, a death's head, with eye sockets fixed on her.

In the morning she told this to Eduardo's father at the brickyard.
He didn't believe her.

"If it happens, what will I do with all these children to feed?"
she asked him.

He doesn't remember what he said, exactly. He knows he just
went to work at bricks. Of course her death's head vision never

materialized. Something worse would: a clerk in the window shaking his normal head. No, no money order from Brooklyn.

Alejandro lived on the floor next to Eduardo for the same reason as Eduardo: to send enough money home to soften the path when he returned. But every night he reminded himself that he'd never thought he would be here living alone and his wife would be home in Mexico with his children. On most nights he thought of his marriage. He'd married his wife in a civil ceremony with his mother and father present. He wore a shirt and he knew she'd worn a dress, but he couldn't remember what it looked like—you only wore a white dress for a big church wedding. He remembered going with her to the clinic for their first baby. He was there at 6 P.M. and waited with her in one room, where she was monitored, and then she went into the delivery room and he stayed outside. They didn't know whether it would be a boy or girl. Each wanted a *niña,* and that's what they got.

He'd set up an upholstery shop in a room in the house opening onto the street. He had to rent a compressor because he couldn't afford to buy one. He had to borrow or rent other equipment. Air pistols, saws to cut—they would cost another 20,000 pesos.

His biggest job had been for 7,500 pesos. He did the whole room—walls, sofa, love seat, and chairs—in fifteen days, and was very proud of it. Fine. But often he could not get a compressor to rent and he had to tell customers who showed him photos of what they wanted that he couldn't get to them until the week after next.

He had been earning the equivalent of about $150 a week. Alejandro and his wife and her brother talked about Alejandro changing what looked like a bleak future: He was going to earn $150 a week and probably less for all of his life. Alejandro and his wife had been talking of his going to America and had agreed that he could try heartbreak for a year and a half for the money. He could earn enough to buy upholstery tools. Then he could work at home and support a family without sweating blood. But this was not Italy, where the men leave Sicily for seasonal work in desolation and loneliness in the north, in Switzerland even, but return to Sicily at the end of the season. A Mexican going to New York must cross the border like a wanted criminal. No husband could return for a simple visit, and no wife could follow him to New York.

Alejandro's wife, who suddenly realized that she would be alone with the children for a year and a half, had been shaken. Her brother helped make the decision: The only way for Alejandro to give his wife and children a future was to change the order of their living now, and for Alejandro to go to New York.

He'd gotten up at 5 A.M., and his wife went with him on the bus to the Puebla airport. She came inside, kissed him goodbye, and stood alone as he went through the gate to the plane to Hermosillo in Sonora. From there he went across a border that was unexpectedly unguarded that night. Ahead of him was Brooklyn and loneliness.

At Brighton Beach, Gustavo had gotten him a job at $7.50 an hour working construction. His arms soon advertised his work. He has iron bars for upper arms. He is 5 feet 6 inches and 135 pounds or so. He has a mustache and a young smile.

He worked for a builder named Eugene Ostreicher and his son, Richie. They were doing a lot of housing in one section of Brooklyn called Williamsburg.

CHAPTER THIRTEEN

Mariano, who slept on the other side of Eduardo in the room at Brighton Beach, came from the house directly behind him in San Matías. His mother and her family kept pigs in pens outside their adjoining cinder-block huts. Anytime they came up short on food, they yanked one of the pigs out of the pen, slit its throat, and went on a steady diet of pig meat. Visitors were happily fed because there wasn't an ice cube in San Matías to keep the carcass unspoiled. If the children became tired of the diet, that was their worry; they could show their ribs. If the pig meat ran out for all, then everybody had rib cages sticking out.

In Brooklyn, Mariano worked at Kentucky Fried Chicken. He didn't know the street it was on, only how to get there. He didn't know what he was going to do when he wasn't working in the afternoon, much less tomorrow. He was single but couldn't go near the topless bars and whorehouses on Fifth Avenue. Lucino Hernández, at thirty-one the oldest in the group, told everybody that the Fifth Avenue bars were dangerous because they get raided by police and anybody without papers could wind up being deported at the flash of a badge.

When they were not out of the house for work, they stayed in their room and watched shows on the Spanish-language stations or talked or slept. On Saturdays they drank. As none of them had a paper to show anything more than name and address, they were inordinately afraid of immigration agents, who in their minds were everywhere. Each day there were reports of a white immigration van on a street somewhere in Brooklyn. When they were walking to work, the impulse was to say something to a pretty young woman, but it was Lucino who always stopped them.

"She might call the police," he said. The police would not bury them in jail for harassing some woman, but they surely would call the immigration agents. And for telling a young woman that you want to get next to her, you would be back in the worst of the dust in Mexico, sent there broke.

It was surer and safer to walk around the corner to Neptune Avenue and toward Coney Island Avenue and run into one of the many whores who were out there every night.

For his first dinner in the house, Eduardo came to the big kitchen table and sat. Around him, everybody was eating and getting up to go to the stove and then returning to the table. He watched them and wondered when his plate would be put in front of him.

There was a discussion about a group of students who were black and who had come out of the high school across the street. They had called Alejandro "Mexican shit." Alejandro said he pretended not to hear them.

"That was the right thing to do," Lucino said. "The Negro. You get in a fight with them, the police come, and then you are fucked. They don't have anything to worry about. They are citizens. You have no ID. They send you back to Mexico."

Eduardo decided that he would never go out of the house except to work.

At that point, he had not worked for a single day yet. He had barely been around the neighborhood. Yet skin color, which was never an issue in San Matías, now touched everything. Already he was aware of the quick, short glances of the whites as he passed them, particularly the white women. And he was learning that the black people didn't like him, and of course he didn't like the looks of them, either. The Puerto Ricans sneered at the Mexicans. The Puerto Ricans didn't like the Dominicans, either, but they most disliked these Mexicans.

"Incas and Mayans! Little people with straight hair!" said Herman Badillo, the first Puerto Rican elected to Congress and now the head of the City University of New York system. "When they speak of La Raza, they don't speak Spanish, they speak in indigenous languages. They should be in separate classes."

Eduardo looked around again for his food. In his whole life, he had never served himself. The mother's hands were always close: one on his shoulder, the other putting his food in front of him.

"What are you looking for?" Martha said.

Eduardo shrugged.

"You get your own food," Martha said.

He got up. He didn't like it. Eduardo's first Saturday night in Brooklyn was the same as the ones that would follow. He was in a commune of the lonely. All week, they worked and came home to eat and sleep so they could work tomorrow. On Saturday night, they preferred being drunk. Lucino wanted them to stay in one loud room while they did this. His brow furrowed whenever somebody said they wanted a bar with women. All he could think of was police walking him to the border and throwing him back into Mexico. Stay here, he said. So each Saturday night, everybody stayed in the room and drank big cold beers, Corona and Heineken with lime twists wedged in them. After every third beer they had tequila. The belief of people from Puebla was that three big cold beers caused an indigestion that only tequila could calm. They got good and drunk and talked about going back to Mexico, where they would climb all over the girls.

Eduardo listened and laughed. He drank a couple of beers but not much else, and this left him as the only one in the crowded room able to deride their fantasies. Alejandro, Gustavo, and Miguel were married and had lived faithfully with their wives and families back home. The religion was in them deep enough to keep them out of adulteries.

"How could you do this to these girls?" Eduardo asked them.

They all called out over the alcohol that not only would they do what they said to these girls, but that they would go far beyond that.

"How can you do that if you don't know any girls?" Eduardo said.

As the night grew late, the laughter turned into the silence of homesickness. Alejandro's wife and two children were living with his family at number 29 Avenida Cinco de Mayo in Santa Barbara, Mexico. He told Eduardo that he imagined his children out at a party. A fiesta. The children are playing while he is talking to everybody at the party. The band is playing *cumbia* music, a mixture of Mexican and Colombian. Then he said he was thinking of all the times he went out with his wife and visited relatives. Dropping in. Nothing formal. There are so many cousins in each family that they take the place of friends.

Eduardo thought of his mother and father, and then the store. He told everybody about the store, as if the video game machine was the attraction, not Silvia, the owner's daughter.

EDUARDO LIVED in local history.

On a larger scale, sociologists first traced Mexican immigration to New York through the Twenty-third Street YMCA in Manhattan, where in the 1920s a small number of people recently arrived from the state of Yucatán established a social club. For some reason, that particular migration ended, but studies of it did not. As there is no way to jump in and out and question some immigrant who doesn't even keep his name on his person, any realistic study must come from a large school, with professors who have a year or two off to work on the project, with papers gathered from everywhere and researchers with the time and funds to travel. Still, it is work done over the longest of hours and you must fall in love with the subject.

The work now is being done by a young professor, Robert Smith, of Barnard College in New York. In a crowded office in Milbank Hall, he writes papers about Mexicans who come to us across the hot sands of an empty desert. On the street outside his window, 116th Street and Broadway, there rise the sounds of New York City traffic at its steadiest and heaviest.

Robert Smith does work that will help so many understand. Others will make a living from his work. He gets a satisfaction that he realizes in the small of the night. He would never trade his life for money.

Two men from a farm south of Puebla live in Professor Smith's studies as the men who started the Mexican migration to New York. They were Don Pedro and his brother Fermin. They had attempted to bribe local Mexican officials and a hungry American bureaucrat to get a contract for the Bracero program that between 1942 and 1964 recruited Mexicans to work in U.S. agriculture. The American sneered at the size of the bribe offer, and the brothers were shut out. They then walked across the border, which at that time, on July 6, 1943, was virtually unguarded. The brothers got on the road and hitched a ride with a man named Montesinos, who was coming from an annual vacation in Mexico City. After talking to them during the long ride to New York, Montesinos thought he could get them started. He put them up at a hotel in Manhattan for two days while they looked for work. At that time, during World War II, anyone could get a job anywhere, and both brothers did. They started

sending money home to Puebla. The arrival of a money order in
the town was an event comparable to none other because money
describes itself. It is money. Its presence in the hands of the relatives
of brothers Don Pedro and Fermin caused others to follow, first in
small groups who crossed uncontrolled borders and survived desert
and river and, once arrived, ran their palms over the sidewalks of
New York, feeling for gold.

By 1980, as many as forty thousand Mexicans had slipped
through to New York for the Job. In 1986 there was an amnesty
that allowed immigrants to apply for temporary residency, then
permanent residency, if they had been living in the United States
since 1981. Immigrants who had been unable to leave New York—
they had beaten the border once, and most didn't want to try
again—suddenly found they could leave the country and return
whenever they wanted. They carried messages home about the
wonders of New York. Some even told the truth: that it was hard
work for higher pay than in Mexico, but low pay for the expensive
city of New York.

The number of immigrants rose to 100,000 by 1990. Ten years
later, there would be an estimated 2.3 million Latinos living in New
York City, with Mexicans the fastest growing of all, at about
275,000. The movement of Mexicans from Puebla and the sur-
rounding towns of San Matías, Atalixco, and Santa Barbara has
accounted for 120,000 coming into the city. There is a large
Dominican population in the city, as high as 500,000, most in the
Washington Heights neighborhood. But there are a mere 8 million
people in the Dominican Republic, as compared to 100 million in
Mexico. Smith's research showed that Mexico needs between
800,000 and 1 million jobs to support its growing populace. Of
course so many would try coming here.

As Smith worked in his office, he did not notice the paper rustling.
His pages about the Job came alive on the street below. Five blocks
down Broadway, Raymundo Juárez, sixteen, and his father had jobs

in a supermarket on Broadway for $6 an hour. They thought it was millions. While the father swept the floor upstairs, his son was crushed to death in a basement compactor. They carried the body out through the basement, and the father never saw the dead son. Now the father stared at a large glass window in the medical examiner's office on First Avenue in Manhattan and a screen over the window went up. The son, Raymundo Juárez, his face swollen, the eyes closed, was on a gurney against a blue cinder-block wall. "*Sí,*" the father said, sobbing. Then he and the cousins ran to a car and drove uptown. They were asked where they were going. "To the store. The store owes his pay," a cousin said.

THE HOUSE EDUARDO came to in Brighton Beach is in an old, crowded part of Coney Island. Coney Island is known for roller coasters and midgets and hot dogs and huge crowds on its wide beaches that run into the Atlantic Ocean. The ocean runs up against so much land at its edges, from New Jersey to the miles of Brooklyn and Staten Island, that the waves generally are small and the currents slow. The people duck and swim a few strokes in bays between old jetties. At one end of the island is Sea Gate Village, residences that are behind gates that keep out cheap day bathers. Sea Gate has its own lighthouse. Coney Island proper now runs past public housing, the super rides, hot dogs, and hot corn; the boardwalk ends at the large and famous New York Aquarium. All after that is Brighton Beach. The oceanfront is tighter, the streets lined by a crowd of five- and six-story apartment houses. The main street, Brighton Beach Avenue, is one block up from the ocean. The aorta of New York civilization, an el line, runs over the avenue. It is the last stop on the Brighton line. Also using this station is the F line, which runs as an el through Brooklyn and after that plunges underground to become a subway. It runs for twenty-five miles, under the wealth of mid-town Manhattan, through a tunnel under the East River to residential Queens, and out for miles almost to the beginning of suburban

Nassau County. There is no ride in the world this far at this price, a dollar-fifty.

Under the el in Brighton Beach, cars are double-parked, often triple-parked, by Russians. At the curbs, the street is a bazaar of Russians selling matryoshka dolls. They begin with a wood peasant woman that unscrews, and inside is a smaller woman, and inside this doll is another, and three or four dolls later, it ends with a peasant woman the size of a thumb.

The sidewalks are under the control of women with shopping carts who stop in the middle of the sidewalk to talk to each other for as long as they feel like it, while people edge by one at a time. The stores sell everything: children's clothing, fruit and vegetables, meats, luggage, shoes. The signs are in Russian, in the Cyrillic alphabet. The stores are crowded and difficult to enter and leave. Push a woman and see what happens.

The streets running north, away from the ocean and the el, have mostly small low wood bungalows that were once summer houses in a resort town. But all this ends suddenly at featureless streets of brick attached houses sitting between old frame houses. Here is the start of a large colony of Mexicans, with young women who work in knitting factories and young men out on street corners for any manual labor. The first small bare Mexican restaurants are on the avenues. And prostitutes appear, of any race, not necessarily Mexicans. At the last of these streets, across from Grady High School, is the house where Eduardo and the other Mexicans lived. At one corner of the block is a small park that has basketball courts.

After that, on the other side of the high school, is a highway, and on the far side of that starts the long march through Brooklyn, miles of blocks, miles of people in a borough whose population nears three million.

Since 1970, Brighton Beach was an area of immigrant Jews from Eastern Europe and Russia, mainly from Odessa, which is exactly like Brighton Beach, a city on the shore of waters that do not get stormy. So many Russians came to these streets that in the Russian national referendum of 1993, the Moscow Central Elections Commission declared Brighton Beach an election precinct. The Russian consulate in Manhattan sent representatives to conduct balloting in a crowded room on the second floor of 606 Brighton Beach Avenue, the meeting room of a Russian military veterans organization and the office of an accountant who prepares American income taxes. Only people who were still Russian citizens were allowed to mark paper ballots for an election in which one candidate was Boris Yeltsin. "You cannot vote for Yeltsin. You are an American. You must vote for Clinton," they said to one man.

Five Russian bureaucrats, two women and three men, supervised the balloting. They writhed because they could not smoke. In Moscow, this balloting would be done in cloud banks from cheap Russian cigarettes.

After forty-five years of the two countries testing atom bombs to make sure they could perform as scheduled over Broadway and Red Square, after all these years of hate and fear, with all of it over different political systems, bureaucrats from Moscow sat in Brooklyn and supervised an election in Russia.

ALEJANDRO TOOK EDUARDO up to see the avenue and the train station. Alejandro knew his way around by subway. He would tell people, "Just tell me where you want me to meet you, and I can get there."

At first, the subway must have been a marvel to Alejandro, but his face never registered astonishment. Then others were the same. Looking for work, or working, occupied their minds so much that they couldn't capture the enormousness of the difference between their lives in Mexico and their lives in New York. Work and drinking were something recognizable and central. Beyond that, Alejandro was fatalistic about the drudgery of work. The trains were not wondrous, he told Eduardo. They were something you used to go to work. Eduardo, who understood work, agreed.

Alejandro told Eduardo how they took the train to the station called Smith/Ninth Street and transferred to a Williamsburg train. Eduardo tried to memorize what he was being told. But we will be on a different train right now, Alejandro said. We are going to be on the Sea Beach line that takes us up to Fifth Avenue in Sunset Park, where everybody is Hispanic. On the train, Alejandro showed Eduardo the transit map on the wall. The train rocked as Alejandro pointed out the lines: B, D, F, N. On the route map they were long lines—highways—in different colors with the stops noted. Often two and three lines used the same stops for at least a while. The M was dark brown, the F an orange line, the B a darker orange, the Sea Beach a light yellow. On the map the Sea Beach line reaches a fork at the Fifty-ninth Street stop and one yellow line mixes in with the light orange and dark orange and the other remains a single yellow line on a field of white. Eduardo still looked at the map in confusion when Alejandro poked him and they got off at the Fifty-ninth Street stop.

Up on the street, Brooklyn's Fifth Avenue was a two-story street of Hispanic signs and shops and Dominicans and Puerto Ricans, but the dominant group, more so each day, was Mexicans. Three blocks over, on Eighth Avenue, suddenly there is the city's second Chinatown, the blocks and blocks of people shining and proud of their growing numbers. Eduardo bought a dark sweater with a hood attached.

Back in the house in Brighton Beach, he looked at himself in the bathroom mirror and was so pleased with the sweater that he put it on the next morning and went out in the steamy August day to the el on Brighton Beach Avenue, so he could learn the route to work. It was too hot to wear the sweater, which he put on the seat next to him. He stood up and swayed and tried to read the map. Suddenly the train stopped at the Smith/Ninth Street station. He remembered being told about this one. He jumped out of the train, forgetting his sweater, and went to the other side and took the train back to Brighton.

It wasn't until he walked into the apartment that something felt like it was missing. Immediately Eduardo clutched his shirt. His sweater was gone. In his mind's eye, he saw it on the subway seat where he'd left it.

He turned around and without a word went back up to the el. He would look for the train that had his sweater. Somewhere there would be a terminal where he could find the train he had been on and come upon his sweater. Some 360 trains come in and out of this station each day. His new train moved, the stations went by, the hour passed. At the last stop, with buzzers and a shush of air, the train emptied. He looked outside for a second train. There seemed to be none. Behind him, a motorman walked up to what had been the last car of Eduardo's train and now became the first car. Eduardo asked the motorman about the first train with his sweater aboard, but he couldn't make himself understood. When the train started he rode a couple of stops, got off and waited for the next train. When this one came in, he walked through the cars looking for his sweater. He found nothing and now looked at the map and didn't know what he was looking at. He asked a Puerto Rican for help. The Puerto Rican looked at the map for three stops and then came up with the route. Secure, Eduardo sat down and stared at the wall. Sand poured into his eyes. He had no idea of the time when he woke up. He asked a doubtful Dominican for directions.

The Dominican said learnedly, "Change at Canal Street."

Two people in the conversation hadn't the slightest idea of where Canal Street was: the Dominican and Eduardo. He did remember being on the train with the lone yellow line on the map. He got off at the last stop and walked. He asked Hispanic after Hispanic, and most were unsure of whether they were in Brooklyn or not.

Eduardo got back to the house some thirteen hours after he left.

CHAPTER FOURTEEN

The New York City Department of Health reported that between 1988 and 1999, there was a 232 percent increase in births to Mexican women. The figures fit the life of the first woman to leave San Matías and make it to New York for the purpose of having children. This was Teresa Hernández, who at eighteen and a couple of months carried the strength of all the generations of suffering that had gone before her.

In the middle of the morning of June 21, 1998, with a sister holding her arm, Teresa Hernández of San Matías came out of her one-room Queens Village apartment in the basement of a frame house. Teresa's husband, José Luis Bonilla, was at his job in a fish market over in the Rosedale neighborhood.

The sister drove her in a battered car approximately seventy-five blocks to the Queens Hospital Center, a large, gloomy orange brick complex on 164th Street and the Grand Central Parkway in the center of what was once old Queens, the Irish and German Queens. Teresa walked into the hospital's main entrance as the advance woman for the new Queens.

With the first cries of her first baby later that morning Teresa saw her child held high in the delivery room lights.

She remembers saying a lot of things about the beautiful baby and her love for her husband. Of course, she maintains that she never for a moment considered the advantages of the baby being born in America as a citizen at first squeal. She says the social worker came through the maternity section and told her about the WIC program, which sees that babies receive free milk. Not until then, she states, does she remember looking at the baby and saying, "American."

She named the baby Stephanie. The name, date, and time of birth can be found in the records of the New York City Health and Hospital Corporation. These show that Stephanie Hernández is an American citizen, and each and every one of her children and her children's children and all who come thereafter will be citizens of the United States. Nowhere in the nation, and probably the earth, has such a large, heavily populated, and important place as New York changed with so many spangles and sounds, with the loudest, highest, and most vibrant a sound no great trumpeter can reach: a baby's first cry.

Teresa gave every young person in San Matías great confidence. She could get to America and then do even more than find a job. In San Matías she remembers dancing at parties in halls; Eduardo was "the one who held up the walls." He didn't know how to dance. She tried to pull him off the wall. "You go to his house and he was always working," Teresa says. "He never met a girl." She saw Silvia at dances, but she was with other boys, not Eduardo.

Teresa Hernández, who went as far as the sixth grade, had never seen a picture of New York or heard anything about it from anybody who went up there. A cousin made it to the Bronx and she waited to hear from him, but he never called. Yet as she scrubbed clothes in an overcrowded room in San Matías, she planned life for children and grandchildren she didn't yet have, and understood how she alone knew how to accomplish it.

She wasn't going to live by the countryside rules for a young Mexican woman. If the girl is pregnant and gives birth at age fourteen or fifteen, the boy just takes the girl and baby away to his mother's home. Only rarely do they take the trouble to get married legally after that. But if the girl is eighteen or twenty and not pregnant, the young man asks her father for her hand and they have a church wedding. However, if they can't afford a big wedding or party, then they don't get married.

Teresa decided to marry José Luis Bonilla without ceremony, for she needed no tiara to prove her status. He was in New York, in Queens, with a good job. He cut up fish, leaving the house at 7:30 A.M. and coming back at 9 P.M. He was working six days a week and earned $400. Sometimes this enormous amount became even larger when people tipped him.

Her emblem of young love would be a pregnancy in San Matías that would end with the baby being born in America, which would produce citizenship for the child and free education and medical care forever. Her husband's visit in July took care of that.

Teresa was eighteen and a half, and six months pregnant, when she left for America in January of 1998. She paid a coyote $2,200. For this she received a flight to Tijuana, assistance to cross the border, and a tourist-class ticket from Los Angeles to New York. Her husband put up the proceeds from scaling ten thousand fish. Teresa says the price was worth it, especially because she was pregnant. She defends the coyotes at each mention. She says they risk jail and, worse, having their trucks confiscated by the border guards. If she had a passport, the journey from Tijuana would consist of stepping across a line and going on to anyplace in America that she felt like seeing. Instead, for want of a piece of paper, it became hours of trudging through thorns and up a mountain, following a trail that was supposed to take them around immigration police and the Border Patrol.

She was with another pregnant woman, and they stopped frequently to rest. One rest in plain sight of Border Patrol agents was interrupted by arrest. She wound up sitting through the night in the second-floor detention hall at the San Ysidro border control point. They took a video of her. She and about two hundred others who had been stopped watched television they couldn't understand while children ran around and babies cried.

Early in the morning she told the immigration officer in charge of the room that she was having her baby right now! It took about fifteen minutes for them to get her through the gate and back into Mexico. "They say they would lock me up in jail if I tried again."

She was back on the trail at nine that night. The coyote told her to follow him through a dirt tunnel that had been dug in the desert. Many of the tunnels have been built by Mexican engineers for money. One tunnel that ended just yards into America at the Tijuana border was bigger and stronger than anything they had in Vietnam, and those people won a war with theirs. Once through, she walked, walked, stopped and wiped the sand clean of her footprints, and walked on. She knew to pat the sand gently, rather than just sweep it and leave a wide, deep track to see from above.

The Border Patrol in their helicopters couldn't see her trail. She laughs at the boys who don't take the time to sweep carefully behind them and risk getting caught no matter how much they paid a coyote to cross them safely.

Tijuana to Queens took a week, most of it spent in a shack that was called a safe house, and her group sat in it for days until somebody came and took them by truck to the airport in Los Angeles and the flight to New York.

She and Stephanie, the first baby, flew home for Christmas in 1998. She found herself pregnant again. Right after the holiday she put her baby, a citizen of America, on the plane to New York with a woman who had papers. Then Teresa joined a group of twenty at the Tijuana Airport, this time paying $1,500. It was hard on her legs, but she was across the border and to the Los Angeles airport without stopping. Even though she was exhausted, there could be no wall, no guard, no storm from the sky that could stop her from getting to her baby in New York.

She paid half the money to the coyote who took her over the border and the last half to one who works out of Queens and who met her at the airport. She will not discuss him, because she knows she will need him several more times.

In Queens, on the morning of July 27, 1999, she asked the landlord upstairs for a ride to the hospital. There, she had her second child, Jocelyn Hernández.

And again, the records of the New York City Health and Hospitals Corporation attest to baby Jocelyn's American citizenship.

She came to this room in a basement of a house in the Queens Village neighborhood, a block off Jamaica Avenue. You walk down an alley and go through the side door and down a short flight of steps to the basement. Her room is in the front of the basement. She is in a room with her children, Stephanie Hernández, one year six months old, and Jocelyn Hernández, four months old.

It is a frame house, like the others on the street, and once was the home of the Queens Irish and Germans. The room has one window high on the wall. There is a small closet. There is a bed that she puts the baby on during the day.

The older child walks around the room. There is a box of toys that she pulls things from. There is a stroller. There are two chairs and a cabinet with a television set on it. In the next low-ceilinged room, a man who rents the space is asleep on a bed against the wall. The rear of the room is a kitchen and refrigerator. On the right is a door to the bathroom. She thinks her single room is a palace.

No matter what happens, she says, I have given them American citizenship.

THE SONG OF Williamsburg was played by thousands and thousands of feet on the wood planks of the walkway on the Williamsburg Bridge, one of three gray iron bridges crossing the East River from lower Manhattan to the borough of Brooklyn. The bridges turned Brooklyn into the fourth largest city in the nation.

The Brooklyn Bridge steps out of the sidewalks and streets around City Hall in Manhattan, climbs gracefully over the East River, and descends to Borough Hall and the civic center of Brooklyn.

The bridge on the left, the Manhattan Bridge, starts only blocks away on the downtown East Side, in Chinatown, and spans the river and drops into a Brooklyn of factories that work weekends.

The Williamsburg Bridge is a few blocks farther uptown. It rises gray and is covered with stiffening trusses, steel latticework whose hundreds of strands give the bridge its industrial appearance and its strength. Out of the famous Jewish tenement streets on the Lower East Side, Eldridge and Orchard and Rivington and Ludlow, the dreary bridge breaks into the sky over the river and slopes down to crowded Williamsburg, a place where children used to go to work.

When it started, when there was no bridge, Williamsburg had about a hundred thousand people who lived and labored in the harshest turn-of-the-century conditions. Of course there were the rich Germans, Austrians, and Irish, who had a pillow wherever they sat. There were such grand people as Commodore Vanderbilt, who stole railways, Jim Fisk, and William C. Whitney.

They were in large houses on streets of expensive hotels and clubs. Along the riverfront they established Pfizer Pharmaceutical, Astral Oil (which soon became Standard Oil), and Flint Glass (which turned into Corning Glass). The rich loved to stroll past their big moneymaking plants and enjoy the sight of the river and Manhattan's glorious Wall Street area. Even more, they loved Williamsburg because it encouraged the true American dream, cheap labor.

From the sitting rooms and porches and lawns of the great houses, it was fascinating to watch the bridge rise. Up from these tenements across the river it began its climb on November 7, 1898. Invisible at first, but soon in plain sight, were the first boatloads of workers out on the river, with pile drivers and high stacks of steel floating on barges.

The bridge took five years to build. With two anchors 2,200 feet apart, the length of the bridge and approaches was to become 7,308 feet. The towers grew to 310 feet above high water, the center of the bridge clearing high water by 135 feet. Suspension cables were $18\frac{3}{4}$ inches thick. The bridge was completed on December 19, 1903, with the cost reaching $30 million.

It was not a handsome bridge, but the idea of bringing together a city yearning to dominate the world was thrilling at first.

And then the song of Williamsburg burst forth.

Here they came across the bridge, thousands and thousands pounding the bridge walkway planks to create a concert, these black hats and beards and anxious dark eyes swathed in babushkas, who rushed in the early-morning darkness to be first to reach the newest of the new land. Soon they would be on trolley cars running across the bridge and immediately after that on subway trains so crowded that choking was part of breathing. The bridge became known as the Jews' Bridge. Those crossing were thrilled by the openness of the streets and the rumors of apartments that were said to be larger than the matchboxes of the East Side. Eyes bulged with astonishment when they saw actual private houses on some of the streets.

Of course they never saw the homes of the rich, but the rich heard their song.

Jews!

The song of Williamsburg came through the air with such force that Commodore Vanderbilt clapped his hands over his ears and swore. No longer would there be a way to maintain his clearing in the social rubble. These people will crush us underfoot! He reached for his walking stick and greatcoat and was out the door with butler and footman, who rushed him by coach out of Williamsburg and home to Fifth Avenue in Manhattan, where he belonged. He would not return. Immediately thereafter the others fled, Whitney and Fisk and such. Williamsburg was left to the grubby commoners in black hats and babushkas who climbed staircases and spilled and shoved into apartments that turned out to be only slightly larger than those they came from, but still allowed perhaps one more pair of shoulders, bunched like a goat's, into the kitchen.

The Vanderbilts, who were the first to flee Williamsburg, became the last family out to buy everything in New York. They lived on Fifth Avenue in a mansion that was big enough to guard the Baltic straits. Partly because of the avalanche of the unwashed in Williamsburg, they wanted Fifth Avenue as a front lawn, and attempted to buy all the land on Fifth Avenue from Fifty-first to Fifty-seventh Streets. When there were complaints from citizens, a Vanderbilt announced, "The public be damned." But the Vanderbilts woke up one morning to find two new hotels going up. Next was a clothing store. They moved farther uptown.

The Williamsburg neighborhood at this time was cut like a map of foreign countries. A neighborhood of Jews ran into one of Italians just off the boat. The Italians had just caused the Germans to move over to the adjacent Bushwick section. Included here was Henry Miller, who was raised for a time on Fillmore Place, off Roebling Street, in Williamsburg, and whose recollections of Ainslie Street were in his writings, which burst forth and shook and shocked the poor constricted authorities of the times. They could not see *Tropic of Cancer* becoming a book that would last forever as a world classic.

Then there were the streets of the Irish Catholics, who were sure that theirs was the only faith and blood, yet the lasting work was done by a daughter of German immigrants, Elizabeth Wehmer, who went to Williamsburg public schools for eight years and left at the age of fourteen. Thereafter, she was described as being autodidactic, which means she taught herself, and at least a generation of newspaper writers who at first thought it meant brain damage used the word to describe her in the ton of stories about her over the many years. In 1943, using her married name, Betty Smith, she wrote *A Tree Grows in Brooklyn,* a novel that pierced the sky over the neighborhood, city, and country as the finest of American letters and emotions.

About that time, there arrived in the harbor a ship with a glorious figure, a rabbi from Romania named Moseh Teitelbaum. It was he who placed the soul of Jewish survivors forever into the crowded buildings of Williamsburg. Reunited with his people, he found only twenty-five of his sect, Satmar, left from the war. They stood on the dock and waved. He stood at the rail and waved back. They waved more. He waved back. It was that way for two days. Teitelbaum made his entrance to America on the holy day of Rosh Hashanah, but under his religious laws he couldn't leave the ship until the observance was over.

The Satmars were people who lived in Romania in the town of Satu-Mare, which means St. Mary. The Jews called the place Satmar, which means nothing except they were not going to say Saint Mary. Before the war, there were several hundred thousand living in and around Satmar, including Moseh Teitelbaum, the rabbi so famous in Eastern Europe, he was the Jew the Nazis wanted first. He disappeared into crowds of his people, and by the time he was rounded up, he was just another Jew with a number. They threw him into the Klausenberg concentration camp. When a man named Kastner bought a train and then paid ransom for Jews to fill the train and go to Switzerland, Teitelbaum, unknown to the Nazis, was one of the first to be let go for money.

When the war ended, Rebbe Teitelbaum went to Israel, saw the whole place destitute, and came to New York to raise funds. He intended to return to Israel, which he saw as a place to live but not a state. His belief was that there could be no Messiah until Israel was made up only of Jews. Any Palestinians living on these lands only delayed the appearance of the Messiah. Other Hasidic sects in Brooklyn believe that the Torah tells them there will be no state until after the Messiah arrives.

Once he could leave the ship, Rabbi Moseh Teitelbaum went first to the East Side of Manhattan and, after that, over the Williamsburg Bridge. His were the footsteps that sent the song of Williamsburg highest into the sky. The moment he arrived in Williamsburg, he was there for good. His group of twenty-five Satmars had eluded the gas ovens and survived dogs and guards' clubs and the sound of firing squads and children's screams. Hundreds of thousands of their sect had died; they lived. After that, handfuls more came from Europe on old freighters, these people who had somehow survived, and now were drawn to the leader whose name was a flame through all the nights in all the concentration camps.

Hasidic groups in Williamsburg now included the first of survivors from Hungary and Romania and Poland, members of the Lubavitch, Bobov, Stolin, Ger, Belz, and Puppa orders. Even at its zenith, with every day starting with the incomprehensible fact of freedom, life in Williamsburg was still trying. They first worked in knitting factories for 25¢ an hour and crowded into the sparse apartments for $3 a month.

Each Satmar couple had an average of six children. The original twenty-five Satmars, reinforced by stragglers, grew to fifty thousand in Brooklyn and over thirty thousand in the suburban Orange County town of Monroe. The Satmars created their own schools in Brooklyn with fifteen thousand students. The sight of children walking into school was a far greater monument to the courage and spirit of the Satmars than all the inscriptions placed on all the buildings. Just as Betty Smith's tree grew and multiplied, so the Satmars spread to become a significant population.

Other Hasidic groups grew as rapidly. The average couple had a minimum of five children and more likely ten. The men had side curls and wore black coats and hats, and the women had their heads covered. Only those in one of the neighborhoods could tell one group from another by their dress. The Puppas wore tall, wide hats, homburgs, with no fold in the top. There was an indentation that seemed punched in with a fist. The hat was Hungarian. The Satmar wore flat hats, a flying saucer from Romania. All wore long black coats and black suits.

They place this barrier of custom between their lives and the world outside, and parts of their customs are looked at skeptically, particularly the covered heads at all times, and in the case of women, the wearing of a wig, or *sheitl;* simultaneously, the face of the woman is open for all to see and admire. For the men, the hat is protection against cold.

Hasidic custom forbids them to shake hands with a woman, which causes them to flee from any woman whose hand is outstretched. But their clothes are the armor of any Hasidic political movement. At election time in Williamsburg, they line streets with as many as two thousand, with the sameness of their black hats and coats and side curls making it appear that there are tens of thousands. In Borough Park, Hasidics fill one street for a rally. The politician on the stage thinks the crowd extends for a mile.

"Our voting is massive," Rabbi Shea Hecht announced one night. He alluded to tens of thousands, but the actual number in the Satmar area on election night was thirty-five hundred or so, and in another Brooklyn area, that of the Lubavitch, there were the usual three thousand.

Somebody running for mayor of New York never sees the numbers, just the hats. There is no time to stop and make a campaign promise to the Hasidim. This is not a labor union with a single demand. The Satmars open with schools, hospitals, and police. Nor are they all that anxious to begin bargaining. As a politician is at his most vulnerable in the haze of victory, the thing that stands out most sharply in recollection is all those black hats. Now, one after another, the black hats walk into City Hall or municipal offices where they want something done. If the mayor is a Roman Catholic, like Giuliani, he bows because he thinks anything else will be interpreted as anti-Semitic.

"We feel we are at our strongest when we come to the mayor after the election," Isaac Benjamin was saying one day. Benjamin often speaks to newspapers and television for the Satmars. "Anyone can get a campaign promise. We get government action."

The mayor doesn't know one Hasid from the other, but he throws himself into every set of arms and pledges his love forever. Much more than that. He summons assistants and orders them to handle any contract one of these rabbis—his best friends in the whole world—hands out. Giuliani placed an assistant, Richard Schairer, into the police department as a liaison to the Jewish community, meaning the Hasidim. He then made a campaign fundraiser, Bruce Teitelbaum, Chief of Staff, who would be helpful to all the needs of the Hasidic community.

Not once would these politicians, who are supposed to carry the last election figures in their hearts, realize that they picked up the same three thousand or so votes that the guy before them received, and that in their own areas the Hasidim could not defeat a black state assemblyman, Al Vann, and that someday soon the Hispanic vote would bury everybody.

Still, you get a non-Jew—and particularly a Roman Catholic—in office in New York, and here is what he says: What is it that you're talking about? You're trying to tell me that they do not exist, that I can't see all those black hats? If I listen to you and ignore them, every one of them will be an enemy, and you tell me how I get reelected then.

As part of publicity for a Central Park concert, Garth Brooks, the country singer, came to City Hall to meet the mayor. Entering the office, he noticed the most prominent picture, that of Giuliani surrounded by black hats. Brooks' eyebrows went up. "I didn't know you had Amish in New York," he said.

THE GREAT TEMPTATION of cheap labor rose out of factories that attracted more cheap labor, Puerto Ricans, into the neighborhood.

They first came on a ship, the *Marine Tiger*, huddled against the winter cold in the first heavy jackets of their lives. Summer people in winter clothes. Soon they were arriving on late-night flights from San Juan, *kikiri* flights—the flight of the chicken. An expressway was built that cut Williamsburg into two sections and destroyed twenty-two hundred units of low-cost housing. The city's answer was to sweep up all the poor and put them into huge high-rise housing projects. This was first done in ancient Rome when all the poor came in from the countryside and authorities built the first high-rises in the history of the world. After a while, the poor hated them and set fires. As municipal corruption in Rome had no bounds, the firemen wouldn't come unless the chief was paid. The buildings were adjudged a failure, and the high-rises for the poor were no more. In New York, two mayors in a row who had gone to Yale, Wagner and Lindsay, put up more high-rises for the poor than the world had seen. They were supposed to have studied things like this in school.

The projects in Williamsburg started a clash between Satmars and Puerto Ricans over who got the most apartments. In late December of 1970, Satmars boarded yellow school buses and went to City Hall, where three thousand in their black hats and great round fur hats demonstrated. Meanwhile, the Puerto Rican women rushed the projects and in the lobbies they put up huge Christmas trees. When the Satmars returned and were confronted with this blaze of lighted trees, there was the beginnings of a riot. Somehow, it was established that the Satmars would have apartments on the first three floors because they cannot use elevators on their holy days and the Puerto Ricans would live all the way into the sky. The Satmars and other Hasidim began a thirty-year push to get the land and housing they needed. One of those days in the future was to make a local builder named Eugene Ostreicher an important man in Williamsburg.

CHAPTER FIFTEEN

Outsiders, particularly anybody nonwhite, assume the Satmars have tremendous wealth. It is at least overrated. In street talk, most Satmars don't have forty dollars. In Brooklyn, the "economic boom" is something to be read about in the newspapers.

"Am I supposed to be burdened by my fortune of money?" Isaac Benjamin was saying in his hardware store on Church Avenue. Whenever anything happens that puts Satmars in the news, Isaac Benjamin is the one everybody calls. He bought the store by promising the owner, David Kramer, as he was dying, that he would take care of Kramer's son, George, forever. The son is autistic and has a photographic memory. He also yells at people when they walk in. Kramer died, Isaac took over the store, and now he stands behind the counter and Kramer's son, middle-aged, yells as you come through the door. He walks to the window and looks out at Church Avenue's traffic. A truck goes by. "Ralph Avenue!" he calls out. That is the address on the truck.

"If he is here thirty years from now, he will tell you Ralph Avenue," Benjamin says.

Kramer's son comes back from the window.

"Birthdays," Benjamin says. "He knows everybody's birthday."

"What's your birthday?" George Kramer asks. "October seventeenth? Same as Christine's. Isaac's is November seventh. Same as my friend Etta Wagner. She's in the Hebrew Home for the Aged, the Bronx. Fifty-nine-oh-one Palisades Avenue. Goldfine Pavilion, room one-fifty-seven. Al Wagner lives in Boynton Beach, Florida. Fifteen Victoria Road. His birthday is June tenth."

Benjamin has read of tax breaks to Pergament and Home Depot and vast riches for all big stores. He fights it out in Brooklyn at full taxes and with Kramer's son still yelling at the customers. He tries to keep up with all matters Satmar.

"Nobody knew," he said. He was talking about the builder Ostreicher. This stocky man came here from Hungary in 1951 and became a citizen in 1956. He started by putting in flooring for supermarkets and then went into general construction in Williamsburg and upstate New York Satmar communities.

"We never knew anything about him except that he let himself be giving to charity. Yeshivas were enjoying his fruits. At dinners he was always a sponsor. Rabbi David Neiderman. Herb Siegel of the city Housing Preservation Department. On Hooper Street near the firehouse he built a yeshiva and a shul. In Monroe he did the same thing. How did he begin? I think he started in floor tiles. Construction, his children took him into construction. How do you get into construction? You go in, you learn how to read prints, and then you're in construction, I guess. We didn't know anything except he was a sponsor at dinners."

New York is the only place ever where a landlord receives cheers. Unlike Manhattan, where buildings search the sky and carry the developer's name, Brooklyn buildings are mostly low and carry addresses whose numbers—760 Seventeenth Street—immediately mark a person as one who must use a bridge or tunnel to get to Manhattan. The landlord is absolved if he can use the title of builder. In Manhattan, the city of unimaginable riches, it is the land developers, barterers, lawyers, and lenders who live the most lavishly, are regarded as the most important, and have politicians fawning and begging for their money. The Manhattan builders contribute outlandish amounts in public to candidates—brazenly, too, for they will give $250,000 to each candidate and receive no criticism. They are of the preferred class. The finances of Brooklyn builders are usually much less, but for the 1996 campaign of Rudolph Giuliani, an unknown, Joseph Spitzer, showed up at the treasury with $83,000, an amount that caused people to drop to one knee. Mr. Spitzer gave his address as 1446 Fifty-ninth Street in Brooklyn, the same as Chaim or Richie Ostreicher. A man or woman can come to a candidate with a plan to feed hot lunches to orphans, and another can arrive with good big fresh money. Those with the hot-lunch idea remain out by the elevators while the money guy is in the innermost room being worshiped.

Immediately he becomes known as a great builder.

And those known as builders usually can't drive a nail or saw a board.

Especially Ostreicher. In 1993, complaints were received in the offices of the New York State attorney general about the condition of condominiums purchased from Ostreicher. An associate attorney general, Oliver Rosengart, went and inspected the buildings one morning. The buildings were on the Williamsburg streets where Ostreicher did all his construction. The three-story buildings had openings in the walls, with no fire stoppage. There was a vertical column of wood when there was supposed to be steel. Drainage was pumped from the basement out to the sidewalk, and there it ended. Rosengart said to himself that the houses were not good enough for the West Bank. Rosengart, an engineer and a lawyer, wrote a report that said, "These buildings are by far the worst constructed buildings I have seen in ten years in making these inspections."

Eugene Ostreicher was the first to arrive for a meeting.

"If they don't like the houses, I'll pay them back," Ostreicher said.

"How much?" Rosengart said.

"Twenty-five thousand. That's what they paid me."

In an adjoining office were the four families. Already they had sworn that they had paid $180,000 each.

Rosengart stepped in and told them of Ostreicher's figure.

"Liar!" one of them said.

"Robber!" another said.

Rosengart asked for proof. "Have you got evidence? Show me your records."

He knew the answer. Of course they had no papers to show. Hasidic transactions are made in cash, and in full. Other than a sudden outbreak of diphtheria, nothing will empty a room faster than the first flash of a traceable check. Everyone involved here believed deeply that any check would be scrutinized by the chief accountant of the Internal Revenue Service himself. Money to buy a house was tough enough to earn without having to risk prison by being asked to account for it.

"You can't go to civil court without any records," Rosengart said. "You better go to a rabbinical court."

The closest outsiders can compare this procedure to are the Italian mob sit-downs, where one person made important by his murder statistics hears complaints and delivers irrevocable judgments. However, the four purchasers had difficulty finding a rabbi in Williamsburg who would sit in judgment of Eugene Ostreicher. He was one of the few people who could obtain land and build housing for people who were sleeping on floors and in hallways. So what if some things were wrong with some of his houses? That could be fixed. The important thing was that people should have a place to raise families and a place to worship. It takes a great man to build for them. Therefore, Ostreicher was great.

The house buyers went from one rabbi to the next and finally they turned to Rosengart and said that they would go to his *bais din,* or rabbinical court. At first he refused, only to succumb to the ceaseless tugging from the four buyers. So there came a morning when they sat in Rosengart's office and he was behind the desk with the full power given to him by thousands of years of Jewish law.

"How much did you pay?" he asked the four. He looked at them sternly.

"One hundred and eighty thousand dollars."

"Is that true?" he said to Ostreicher.

"They gave me thirty-five thousand," Ostreicher said.

"He lies!"

"How could you lie like that? You are in a sacred court."

"I'll pay," he said.

"How much?"

"What they gave me. Four hundred thousand dollars."

"He lies again!"

"Seven hundred twenty thousand," one of the buyers said.

"I received six hundred twenty-five thousand," Ostreicher said.

"When will he stop deceiving and lying?" another of the buyers said.

"Which is it?" Rosengart asked sharply.

"Seven hundred and twenty thousand," Ostreicher said finally.

The agreement was reached with both sides seething. They finished at an hour reserved for prayer. Anger was suspended. There were nine, including Ostreicher. A tenth man was needed in order to reach a minyan, the number required for prayer. "You?" they said to Rosengart. He nodded. Why, of course. The long day of distrust, deceit, and denunciations ended in prayer.

However, when Rosengart finally got back to his office, he put the details of the unconscionably bad construction into a file, where it would remain for six years. Then one day an investigator for the government's Department of Labor took the file. It would become the start of a clear fact pattern in a case against Ostreicher.

THE SON, RICHIE OSTREICHER, had spent several years studying the Talmud in a Satmar community in Monroe, New York. Studies in Hebrew schools are at marathon length. His friend Sam Newman, who was there with him, recalls, "We studied fourteen, fifteen hours a day. We got home twice a year. He seemed to like it. I was not too sure. You can see who is going to continue as a scholar. After you come out into the free world, and you still want to study, that shows your desire. Me, I wasn't so much for it. Richie did study once in while."

As the sections of the Talmud are thousands of years old, each section must be scoured and discussed and gone over again and again. Newman says that of course he and Richie studied for interminable hours the rules that no one is allowed to take advantage of an employee, that no employer is allowed to eat until he pays his workers. But this refers to day workers, who put in a hard day and should be paid that night. Workers on a weekly or monthly payroll are different. As for day workers, if a man says he needs the job so desperately that he will work cheap, you shouldn't take advantage of him. Still, he is so desperate for work that at times you create a job for him, and this puts it into a gray area. It isn't right to take advantage of him, but the question is, is it the wrong thing to give him this work right away? After all, you're not God. God is God. The man needs work. But does his need mean you're supposed to pay him more than he'll take? On the street, the answer is a distillation of scriptures: Pay the guy enough so that you can have something under your feet when you stand and claim that you're not robbing him.

In their lives and times of living in the most diverse center of population in all the world—a Brooklyn of people driven off the cotton fields of the South by machines, or from the slums of San Juan and Port-au-Prince and Santo Domingo and the sparse living of Cholula—the Hasidim had the most complicated feelings. They didn't like anybody who wasn't white, don't worry about that. But they couldn't do without them, particularly Mexicans, because they were cheap labor and the world has nothing to rival that, nor has it ever. Then, unlike the non-Hasidic Jews and the Irish and Italian and Germans, the Hasidim did not flee from other races. The Hasidim bought land and houses because they were going to remain in Brooklyn. The Lubavitch grand rebbe, Menachem Shneerson, called it a deep moral obligation not to run from blacks. Others, particularly Catholics, didn't know what he was talking about. They were moving out to Long Island to spend three and four hours a day getting to and from work because they loved the Long Island Expressway so much. The Hasidim regarded themselves as morally superior to these people. They stayed in Brooklyn and called 911 on the blacks and Mexicans at night. In the morning they hired them to work off the books, and for minimum wage—maybe.

WALKING INTO THE temporal world, Richie Ostreicher went immediately to work in his father's construction company. He also became active in the Ninetieth Precinct community meetings. If a cop was sick or injured, Richie was a visitor. He became a cop buff with a yarmulke. The police at first thought he was a local rabbi, but then Richie, by behavior and speech, magnified this illusion into his becoming a police chaplain, and a man of the cloth with this badge can do just about anything and at all times.

Williamsburg is the neighborhood of the Ninetieth Precinct, which is in a gray cement three-story corner building on Union Street. The precinct shares the front of the building with the Fire Department's Battalion Fifteen. Chief John Dillon, short and stocky, with a crew cut, is in charge. The boss over him is Deputy Fire Chief Charles Blaich, who is a critic of the New York City Buildings Department and of the work they allowed to proceed. Blaich began with a degree in chemistry and a master's in protection management, and then kept taking construction courses because all fire department promotion exams have many building questions.

Blaich married Mary DiBiase, who was the photographer for the

New York *Daily News* who climbed a fire escape to get the famous picture of mobster Carmine Galante dead with a cigar in his mouth in the backyard of a restaurant in Ridgewood, Queens. "Don't you look up my dress!" she said to the photographers following her up the ladder. Her photo went all over the world. Now she raises two kids in Staten Island and once in a while gets a call from the *New York Times* and from some Catholic publications. She goes out with her cameras and tells herself, "queen for a day." She bought $6,500 worth of cameras for sports events, and she takes pictures of night baseball games at Yankee Stadium while whatever her family does for dinner, they do it alone.

Around the side of the building is Truck Eight of Police Emergency Services. Upstairs, always on the ready, is Billy Pieszak, out of Our Lady of Czestochowa school, on Thirty-second Street in the Sunset Park neighborhood. During his school days Polish was the first language. His home bar is Snooky's, which everybody in his Brooklyn knows. His best souvenir is a New York City detective badge used to open the show *NYPD Blue*. It was given to him by Bill Clark, who once was a detective in the Ninetieth Precinct and went on to become the producer of *NYPD Blue*.

There was an afternoon when Bill Clark and a television crew were shooting a scene in front of the precinct. A car with police lights and windshield parking placards pulled up, and a heavy guy with a beard and yarmulke got out.

"Bill Clark, *NYPD Blue?* I'm the NYPD Jew," he said.

He introduced himself as Richie Ostreicher. Clark thought he was a Police Department chaplain. If there is one thing that makes an Irish detective back off, it is a Jewish chaplain. Clark, even though retired, did what every Catholic cop ever did, and that was to virtually genuflect. This came from the nights and days of the Satmar's famous Rabbi Wolfe, who was introduced as an untouchable by the Brooklyn commander and who then walked into the squad rooms of the Sixty-sixth and Seventy-first and Ninetieth Precincts and without so much as a grunt of hello went into the confidential files. Detectives typed up notes without looking at him.

Rabbi Wolfe's main need was all accident reports involving Satmars. If, on rare occasions, a Satmar had a criminal matter pending, Rabbi Wolfe studied the complaint, then asked for a match.

After the day's filming, Clark went for dinner at the Old Stand, on Third Avenue and Fifty-fifth Street in Manhattan. Richie followed in his car. As he observed kosher rules, he ate no food. Instead, he had soda and talked incessantly about the police. He said it was "the job," which is how police give their occupation: "I'm on the job." He identified precincts in cop language. It was the "nine-oh," not the Ninetieth. He was engaging and excited about cops. Clark recalls, "He did not have a gun. If he had one, he would have made sure that I was aware of it, that he was carrying. He talked like the construction business was his. But I assumed his father was the show and that Richie just did things for him."

When Clark got back to the Regency Hotel, where he was staying, there were flowers in the room for his wife, Karen, from Richie Ostreicher.

Richie Ostreicher was married on November 25, 1998, and had the reception at the Le Marquis at 815 Kings Highway. The guest list showed Police Commissioner Safir at table fifty-four, Inspector John Scanlon at fifty-five, First Deputy Commissioner Patrick Kelleher at thirty-one, Inspector Vincent Kennedy at thirty-two, Deputy Chief of Patrol William Casey and Chief Tom Fahey at thirty-six, in addition to the mayor's special assistant, Bruce Teitelbaum.

The father had just bought nine lots from the city at an uncontested sale for $345,000. The lots ran the length of a long Williamsburg block, Middleton Street. He intended to build three- and four-story apartment houses.

AT THE SAME TIME the construction work of Eugene Ostreicher was stopped temporarily by the Fire Department, Eduardo Gutiérrez was in and out of stores asking for work. A Korean who had a fruit store on Fifth Avenue in Brooklyn hired him without saying a word. Eduardo knew that the job was seven days a week of twelve-hour days at pay of $250 a week.

Eduardo became another Mexican sitting on a box in front of the flowers and fruit bins outside a market, the immigrant learning that America is a word that also means drudgery.

The United States Department of Labor showed in a survey that a Korean immigrant starting work in New York received $500 a week and a Mexican only $270, which is an unrealistically high figure. Down to the bottom, the lightest skin color does best.

One Korean store owner hired a Korean for $500 and two Mexicans for $230 and $270 a week. When his business slowed, he fired the Korean and one Mexican and hired a second Mexican for $170 a week.

The study showed that the usual Mexican earned $170 a week for a seventy-hour week, the equivalent of 1,700 pesos; there was no such salary in dream or reality anywhere in San Matías.

The Mexican population in the United States has reached six million. They wire home $6 billion a year. This amount is counted on by Mexico's banks. Mexico's credit line with American banks is based on the expected national income from Mexicans without papers in America.

They are in the dark dawn doorways of coffee shops and restaurants, the bread delivery next to them, waiting for the place to open for the start of their twelve hours as dishwashers and porters for $170 for a six-day week.

"Why don't you go to school?" Angelo, the owner, asked José, fourteen, when he presented himself for a job in the Elite Coffee Shop on Columbus Avenue. José asked, "Is the school going to pay me?" Angelo shrugged and he motioned the kid to the kitchen, where he would still be ten years later.

They all put their bodies up.

My friend Maurice Pinzon was on an East Side subway when three Mexicans got on at the stop underneath Bellevue Hospital. One held up a hand that had a white hill of bandages. He cursed the job that caused this. He had lost a finger and the doctors in Bellevue couldn't help. "They throw away my finger like garbage," he said. One of his friends said, "Now you cannot work."

"Why not?" the injured one said.

"How can you drive at work?" one of his friends said.

The guy shrugged. "I drive with one hand."

In Brooklyn, the A train on the old dreary el tracks outside drowned out the crying of the women in the second-floor rooms. The body of Iván Martínez, 17, a brother and cousin to the thirteen people in the apartment, had just been taken off the street and carted to the medical examiner. He was here from Puebla, delivering pizza for $150 a week, when three hoodlums from the neighborhood shot him in the head, took $36, and went for chicken wings from a Chinese takeout.

And Brother Joel Magallan sits in the offices of the Asociación Tepeyac de New York on West Fourteenth Street and talks about the trouble of trying to make it better. "They hired census organizers a year before. They hired Mexicans one month before. We had no chance. The new president of Mexico wants to have a guest worker program. You sign up in Mexico. That means none of the people coming here as guest workers can join a union."

He held out his hands. In the far suburbs of Suffolk County, two Mexicans who stood in front of a 7-Eleven store in the town of Farmingville were picked up by two whites who said they wanted them for day work but instead took them to an isolated place and gave them a beating. Some politicians in Suffolk thought that a central hiring hall would stop violence, but the county executive turned down the idea. He said it would be illegal to put a roof over their heads.

In the room next to Magallan's offices, one of his staff was interviewing a young guy who had been working at a store selling accessories in the Bronx. He worked one hundred hours a week for $200. The boss had tables set up outside the store and wanted the Mexican to work them. "I had a bad cold," the Mexican told Magallan's worker. "He fired me." They had the Mexican get a witness and made out papers for $8,800 in back pay. Maybe there would be this one victory. Maybe not. It is so hard to be on the bottom in New York.

Eduardo Gutiérrez became another of the black and brown who stand in the cold darkness of Bedford Avenue in Williamsburg and wait for someone to pick them up for a day's work. It is his first morning here. He had come to Brooklyn for a construction job, but it was shut down for a while, and the Korean market was a bust, so he was on the street to look for work.

There is no street with the past and present of Bedford Avenue, which starts miles away at hamburger stands and bars around Brooklyn College and crosses Nostrand Avenue to form a space where old men, with cheers still in their ears, tell of the day John F. Kennedy drew a crowd of far over a million in his campaign in 1960.

After the college neighborhood, Bedford Avenue runs into streets almost entirely of color. It is here, a few yards up from the corner of Empire Boulevard, that it goes past high gloomy brick public housing known as Ebbets Field Houses, which stand where the old ball field had the Dodgers as a home team. So few know that it is the place where the most profound social change in the country took place. That was on a raw March afternoon in 1947 when Branch Rickey, the owner of the Dodgers, sent a typewritten note to the press box at Ebbets Field during a preseason exhibition game. "The Brooklyn Dodgers today purchased the contract of infielder Jack Roosevelt Robinson from Montreal. He reports immediately." Thus changing baseball, and the nation, whether it realized it or not. Robinson was the first of color ever to play in the majors. This happened while Martin Luther King Jr. was a sophomore in an Atlanta high school, it was before *Brown vs. Board of Education*, before Harry Truman integrated the armed forces, before Little Rock school desegregation, before the lunch counter sit-ins of the South. Before anything here was Jackie Robinson on first base at Ebbets Field as the first black in baseball. Long years later, during a lecture at the New York Historical Society, Frank Slocum, who had been in the Dodgers office in Robinson's time, was asked how something of such magnitude and complications could have been done with only two sentences, when any decent law firm would compile a foot-high stack of briefs.

"Yeah, but we were really doing it," Slocum said.

Today, the Ebbets Field Houses and the school across the street from it, Intermediate School 232, the Jackie Robinson School, are dreadful proof that one magnificent act becomes just that, one act, when placed against the grinding, melancholy despair of life every day. Cling to the great act that can inspire and give hope. But you can't brush away the effects of the disease of slavery and suddenly make softer the life of thousands of children who come out of the housing project with keys around the neck, latchkey kids, for no one is at home when they return from school. The school has a narrow fenced-in cement yard unworthy of a state prison, a yard with flowers at one end for the young boy who was shot dead while playing basketball. The school is one of the five worst in the city.

Past the housing project, the avenue goes down a long slope, and the color suddenly changes to white and the avenue becomes one of Hasidic Jews, the men with black hats, beards, and long curls, the women with heads covered with kerchiefs.

The four-story brick corner house at number 527 has claws coming out of the foundation. It is the home of builder Eugene and son Richie Ostreicher. On the side is a new addition, a garage for their construction company.

The street goes around a curve and comes up to a park and bodega where Eduardo stands outside, looking for work.

He was in T-shirt, jeans, and sneakers, with his black cap on backward. And he was, like the others standing alongside him, a person of towering dignity. He had put up his young life to come to this curb and look for work to build a house for his future, and to buy book bags for his sisters in San Matías.

He became one of the blacks and Mexicans who waited for people to pull up and beckon to them and take them away for day labor, cleaning lots, emptying trucks, rearranging warehouses. They stand here in their rough clothes and dark skin, mostly unable to speak English, coming from rooms without bathrooms, without kitchens, and if they must walk far to a subway, then they walk far to a subway. In the dimness they may seem like unkempt shadows, but as you watch them, they grow and the features are defined and the heads are raised. They are the aristocrats, descendants of the pure royalty of 1947 of their street. Yes, it happened long ago. And now there still is so far to go. But once you were too far down even to dream. Now, back where Bedford crosses Empire Boulevard, Jackie Robinson hits a single and right away takes a couple of steps off first base and the crowd shouts in anticipation. He is going for second! He is the only player who can cause a commotion just by taking a couple of steps off first. And take the step he does, and take second he does, and when he stands and brushes off the dirt, he becomes the hope for those millions and millions who had gone out each day, as did the generations before them, feeling only the deadliness of despair, believing there was nothing better. He stood for the dawn people on Bedford Avenue who take a step off the curb and peer at the headlights to see if anybody is slowing down to stop and give them work. Bedford Avenue whispers in their ear. Sure, so much is hideous. But the dream has been handed down to them. They take any insult, suffer any degradation, face every unfairness and injustice, yet never leave, because they are here for others, for wives and children at home, and nothing can make them quit.

Here on Bedford, each time a car or van suddenly pulls up and the driver calls "One" or "Two," the number of workers he needs, the street standers rush blindly to the car and go diving into the backseat. They go off without knowing where they are going or how much they are going to be paid. The word *job* throbs through their bodies unconditionally. Those waiting on the curb can be there for the full day. One or two, or at the most three at a time, jump off the fence and run to get a job without questioning. The jostling on the sidewalk is continual and causes despair among those left at day's end.

For all the valor spent chasing work, the Mexicans also are irresistible temptations, the nearest occasion of mortal sin: cheap labor.

It is blood in the mouth of nearly everybody who hires.

That left Eduardo with only one thing to do. He was on the curb at Bedford Avenue by 6 A.M., one of a pack of people trying to feed a family. One or two remember being there with him. One was Rafi Macias, who had had a job for $7.50 an hour at a luggage factory in Long Island City. One Monday when he climbed the factory steps to his floor, the foreman was in the doorway and told him that there was no work. The place had moved. He remembers that his first thought was of his son on a tricycle on the street in front of the housing project in Coney Island. He came right to the curb at Bedford. He remembers that he caught a job that day, cleaning a yard in Hackensack, New Jersey. The guy gave him $60 and that was all right. He didn't return from the curb empty.

Somebody told Miguel Aquino that Italians paid $10 an hour for construction workers, and so he went to Eighteenth Avenue and Sixty-fifth Street in Bensonhurst only to find so many waiting that he was shut out. After that, he remembers trying Utica and Fulton, where Italians in vans were hiring, but when Miguel started for one van, a Puerto Rican punched him on the side of the head, and Miguel lost his balance and the job.

He, too, did not go home. He came straight to Bedford, though it was too late the first day. But he says he stayed because he couldn't face his wife and children at home knowing that he had quit when he should have kept trying.

On that first day on the street, Eduardo missed out on every chance and went home disgusted. He reminded himself that he had to get the jump on them. He was quicker the next day and was out front for a plumbing truck, and spent the day moving pipes. He came home with $45.

Farther along, the street for work, Bedford Avenue, now becomes Puerto Rican. Flags, loud music, Spanish calling through the air. Then the sidewalks turn old Polish and new Eastern European, a street of people smoking furiously in coffee shops with leather jackets tossed over their shoulders. But so many Polish stand under the Williamsburg Bridge and look for work each morning. At North Eighth Street is a subway that is only one stop to Manhattan's East Side, and it is a thousand miles away.

Eduardo took the room's cell phone into a corner of the kitchen and called Silvia in College Station for the first time. She remembers being surprised to hear from him, for she knew that he hadn't asked her mother or father for her phone number. He told her that he got the number from a brother-in-law of her cousin in the Bronx.

"How is work?" she asked him.

He mumbled. She thought later that he didn't want to admit that he had traveled this far to get hit-or-miss work.

She told him that she worked at the barbecue stand in the morning and the Olive Garden at night.

"I make minestrone soup for four hundred and fifty people," she said. She was aware that he didn't know what minestrone soup was, so she told him about cutting up the vegetables for it.

She asked how many people were in his room. He told her six. She thinks that he didn't want to tell her the exact number, eight, because he knew that she didn't like a crowded bedroom.

He asked her how many were in her house in College Station. She told him five, but it was only a two-bedroom apartment and she was used to her own room. Things would be better soon. Finally, he volunteered something. He had done his own laundry.

He had taken all his shirts and underwear to a coin laundry and washed and dried them.

"Make sure you tell that to your mother," she said. "She won't have to do your wash anymore. I won't either."

That got him flustered and the call was over. He said he would call again, and he did. But he made the call when he came home after work and she was just leaving for the night job at the Olive Garden. She could say only a few words. On the next couple of calls, the time difference caused him to miss her. Silvia remembers trying him once on the cell phone and getting no answer.

The next time he called, he said he was working on a construction job. He didn't say much more. He was still strangled by shyness, even when shielded by a phone. By now, everybody in the room at Brighton knew this, and when they all got off the train at Flushing Avenue and walked down the streets to the job at Middleton, they started in on him, did it because he was so easy, just walking there with them.

"Look at the pretty girl, Eduardo," Alejandro remembers saying to him when a woman passed by going to work. "Go up and tell her how pretty she is. Tell her you will die for her."

Eduardo never stopped to think that the others never would do this. They were afraid that the woman would call for the police and get them deported. All he did was look at the sidewalk as he passed the woman. Early on in his days on the job, Eduardo showed that he could not break out of his shyness; nor could he handle the others taunting him about this. One morning he came off the el steps running. He went all the way to the job. He liked the run. It kept them out of his ears. From then on, he ran from the el each morning. Finally, they said that they would stop fooling with him. He did not believe them. Still he ran.

CHAPTER SIXTEEN

The building business in Brooklyn lives on the eighth floor of the seedy old Municipal Building, upstairs from the Court Street stop of the number 2 train. You come off the elevator on the eighth floor only to be blocked by the back of a large woman in a plaid coat who is on one of the three pay phones on the wall.

"Listen, he thinks that because I work around the corner, I can come in here as a favor for noth—" She listened for half a breath. Then she roared, "Exactly! They think I can do this when I go out for coffee. I'm here an hour alread—"

This time she suffered the other voice for a moment, then snaps, "No. Give me Alex. I'll tell him that I want to get paid for this."

A small man in a leather cap is jammed into the wall by the woman. He talks in a low voice on another pay phone.

Inside a cubicle a step away from the phones, three people sit at old computers that rattle. A sign on the wall says each person is allowed ten minutes. Another says, If You Offer a Bible, It Is Considered a Gift.

Next to each computer, a printout machine that could have

carried the news of Truman's victory rattles and grinds as it sends
out long pages of building violations. They are printed too faintly
for all human eyes except for those of the expediter. Without the
expediter, builders couldn't build a doghouse in Brooklyn. These are
hallway people who know computer codes, all Buildings Department regulations, and also the offices and members of the Buildings
Department. The commissioner for Brooklyn, Tarek Zeid, has a wife
who is an expediter. His office was a few yards down the eighth-
floor hallway until he took a leave under some fire.

Expediters gather all the paper a builder needs and do it in a
tenth of the time he could and then move in and out of hallways
and offices and fix anything that has to be fixed. The builder
wouldn't know where to begin.

A rabbi spins around and asks, "What do I do?"

"You got to take a number," he is told. "Take a number like it's
the butcher's."

Three people sitting on chairs ignore the rabbi. Four others are
standing against the wall. Now one person at a computer stands up,
clutching his printouts. Two tumble from the wall and try to get there
first. But a man gets out of his chair and beats them to it. He starts
commanding the computer to find his specific violations. The woman
in the plaid coat from the hallway bursts forward. She yells to
everybody, "You didn't take a number!" She pushes hard. The man
leaving with printouts has to burrow through the people.

One person at the computer, a young law student named Maurice, whose long pointed chin looks as if it could punch a hole in
the keyboard, turns around and says, "This doesn't work."

A man with a face of cigarette smoke and wearing a candy
store sweater, an old maroon cardigan with pockets for change,
jumps off the wall.

"Go back. Punch A. Did you hit A? All right. Hit PUB, then
PRM. That's—"

"I already did."

"Then you're in. You're logged on."

"I'm still not."

"Did you hit three?"

"Three?"

"You want Brooklyn, you press three to get into Brooklyn. Every borough got a different code. Three is for Brooklyn. You want Brooklyn, you just press three and you got Brooklyn."

Maurice nods and presses the key. With Brooklyn up, he taps out the name he was doing research on, Ostreicher. His chin comes closer to the keyboard.

His tutor has gone back to leaning against the wall. The young guy is learning the trade of expediter, which is as essential to the building of a building as the roof.

The printer alongside the young guy now begins to grind out page after page of violations for Ostreicher.

34232893K VIOL ACTIVE

43 LORIMER STREET
RESPONDENT INFO: OSTREICHER, CHAIM 527 BEDFORD
AVENUE, DESCRIPTION OF VIOLATION:

STAIR ENCLOSURE DOES NOT COMPLY WITH THE
REQUIRED FIRE RESISTANCE RATING; IN THAT BUILDING IS
BUILT AS A FOUR-STORY OCCUPANCY GROUP—WHICH
REQUIRES A TWO-HOUR FIRE-RATED ENCLOSURE AS PER
SECTION PFI.

B 5027
STRUCTURAL DEFECTS VIOLATE REFERENCE STANDARD
RS10-5B IN THAT 1.—NO STRAP BRACING FOR FOR "C"
JOISTS II ANCHORAGE BETWEEN JOIST AND BEARING OR
NON-BEARING WALL WAS NOT PROVIDED.

B5C 27
EXISTING APARTMENT DOORS OPEN DIRECTLY INTO
STAIR ENCLOSURE CONTRARY TO D 27 373. REMEDY: FILE
PLANS TO LEGALIZE IF FEASIBLE AND CONFORM TO CODE.

Every ten minutes the person at the machine is supposed to give it up and let the next person look up all his violations. But when Maurice's ten minutes are up, unseen hands push him back down. As the old violations come out of the printer, one of the expediters is offended by Maurice's inefficiency. "How could you let this go on?" he says. "You are supposed to get certificates of correction."

The large woman in plaid snarls, "The engineer has to write a letter. That's work you should have done. Who are you? What are you doing with such a mess?"

After all, their business is to rectify dangers in a building by means of pieces of paper. All this noise from people on the phone, from the world's only noisy computers, from old printers makes it impossible for a person to think of somebody dying in a building. If somebody dies in a fire in a stairwell or falls off the building, that is a tragedy. But these things do not happen every day, and therefore what is of concern is getting the proper certificate so the builder can build.

One expediter prints out complaint number 4069852, filed on September 8, 1997: "Multiple dwelling fire escape in danger of collapse—all rear." The clerks handling the complaint listed it with priority C, which placed the complaint on a level with a missing shingle. That had to please the expediter. Some 339 days later, the Fire Department inspected the premises. Their report said the fire escape was "in danger of collapse and was a health hazard to both the building's occupants and members of the Fire Department." The owner was ordered to fix the fire escape immediately. But if the clerk in the Buildings Department had listed the complaint as priority A, where it belonged, it would have been targeted for inspection in a day and a half.

That a potentially hazardous condition was placed in the wrong priority category was found in twelve complaints out of a batch of seventeen. The response time in inspecting and ordering repairs for these defects—which ran from a corroded I-beam to an unsafe structure—went from the day and a half of a priority A to the weeks and months of other priority classes.

This could be the result of a department with so few inspectors that it is impossible to inspect even the urgent. The priority category is dropped to protect the department workers, with everyone hoping that the conditions won't worsen and people won't get hurt. The change of categories is also a smashing tactic for expediters. Turn the B into a C and tell the owner he can go on vacation.

The first street on Ostreicher's violations list, Lorimer Street, was empty and sullen when Ostreicher first arrived to build. Old closed factories sat on the edges of empty lots. Up ahead was the old yellow el trestle passing by the red brick Woodhull Hospital. Once, when John Lindsay was mayor and the people running the city were young and full of hope, Woodhull was built as a public hospital with all private rooms. It was Lindsay's belief that if people could have a private room in Lenox Hill Hospital because they had the money to pay for it, then the poor should have a private room because they didn't have the money to pay for it.

Lorimer Street backs onto Middleton, where Ostreicher also planned to build.

His streets of brick condominiums—look-alike, in trouble alike—stood for the worst, and they looked up the street at the best.

JOSÉ DANIEL, SEVENTEEN, Eduardo's younger brother, talked to Eduardo several times on the phone about his coming to New York. In March 1999, Eduardo told José that he could get him a construction job. José immediately left San Matías. The coyote price was $1,600. The entire family in San Matías dug hard and came up with airfare to Tijuana, but that was it. José, following the path of his brother, and the others who had gone before him, went to a small hotel in Tijuana called the Azul, where he met the same coyote who had taken his brother across. José arranged to come to New York as a "collect immigrant." His brother would somehow have the money waiting. But as José had not even made a partial payment, he was considered a risk to flee once he was in America. Therefore, he was treated as a suspect through the entire trip. The coyote would have a man take him to New York, where Eduardo would meet them with the money in his hand. Please be there.

José was one of a crowd of twenty young men who followed the coyote for long hours through a desert of bushes and sand. The coyote pulled away bushes that covered the entrance to a tunnel that had dirt walls and ceiling. There were only a couple of wood supports visible. The tunnel was pitch black and airless. The coyote used a flashlight. The ones with him used their fear. José remembers people calling out that they felt a snake. Some tried to turn and go back, but they were going through the tunnel in a chain, and so this could not be done. One raised his voice to a scream. This stopped nothing. When they emerged from the tunnel, José remembers, they walked in the scrub parallel to a highway for a long time. Two vans then picked them up and drove them to a house in Phoenix. He does not remember how long he stayed there. The immigrants with him were leaving one at a time with a coyote. In the late afternoon, a Mexican who had nothing to say grunted and indicated the door. He was burly with uncut hair and wore a black rain jacket. José and three others went with him. A van took them to the Phoenix airport, where they went through the metal detector while the silent coyote walked around it. A Hispanic working at the metal detector nodded. They got on a flight to New York. When the coyote sat, his rain jacket was open and a shirt showed something beneath, gun or knife. The coyote jammed the ticket receipts into his pocket. He spoke for the first time. He told José in short harsh words that his brother Eduardo had better be right on time for their meeting and have the money. He said no more. He was unconcerned about the other three. When the plane stopped at Chicago, they got off without goodbyes.

The flight to New York brought José and the coyote into chilly darkness at LaGuardia Airport. The coyote, who knew the city, took José on a bus. Then they took a subway for some time. José was excited by the noise and lights and speed. He asked where he was. The coyote told him the Bronx. The train then became an el. José stood up and walked to the opposite side of the car in order to see what was behind a bank of bright lights on the ground below. The coyote immediately stood next to him. When José went back to his seat, the coyote was with him. The train stopped and the doors opened, and suddenly the coyote held an arm in front of José. He acted as if he was stopping José from getting off at the wrong stop. He had not come this far to lose a cash customer. As the train was going to the next stop, the coyote showed some tension. He put a hand on José's arm. At the next stop, he guided José out to a platform that was empty. The coyote had a hand close to whatever he had inside his jacket and under his shirt.

There was a call from the middle of the platform. Eduardo was coming off a staircase and walking excitedly through one station light and into the darkness toward them. The coyote pretended to smile, but José remembered that he kept his shoulder in front of him. Eduardo walked up and put his hand into his pocket to get the money. This caused the coyote to stiffen, and his hand dug into his jacket pocket. Then he saw the cash. It now was a straight exchange, immigrant for cash. Suddenly Eduardo and José were afraid that the coyote would take the money and for some reason kill them. They had never thought of such a thing before, but now it was obvious in the night air on the empty platform. The coyote's right hand held the weapon, showing that he was afraid that the two brothers would kill him and keep their money. There had been a series of dead bodies in the Bronx to validate all their fears. Eduardo counted the money out as fast as he could. He then handed it the coyote. This was the instant where murder might take place. The coyote snatched the money with his left hand and walked off in one motion, closing his jacket.

There was no construction work because of the weather. José went to the curb on Bedford Avenue and then was told by Lucino in the room in Brighton Beach about a job at a grocery store on Avenue U, which was within walking distance of the Brighton house. He got the job and worked twelve hours a day, seven days a week, and was paid $240. At the end of each day he sat in gloom. Had he known that he would make such little money, had he known that if he kept a job like this it would take him almost a year to repay the $1,600 to his brother, he would have stayed in San Matías.

Then the weather broke and there was excitement in the room at Brighton Beach. They were going to work, and they were sure they could get José on the job. They did.

Suddenly, he was making $340 a week and he could repay the loan and still send money home. He worked three floors up at the back of the site. Lucino was his partner. Eduardo was on the street side. The brothers rarely talked during work. Afterward they went to the corner bodega and sat in the back and had pizza or chicken or tacos. Then they took the train home. Sometimes they went to a store and bought Mexican vegetables and steak and cooked that at home. Otherwise, nothing changed except the date on the calendar. This drudgery each long day consumed their lives just as would an illness.

Everybody working regarded the structure as unsafe. Eduardo and José talked about this during what both felt was their one best day in New York. They took the subway over to Battery Park and stood looking at the Statue of Liberty.

Eduardo posed while his brother took his picture, and then he took pictures of his brother, and after that they asked tourists to take pictures of both of them. They were proud to show their best shoes, dark construction boots with yellow tops.

They wondered if their youngest brother, Miguel Angel, was carrying more than one slate at a time. He must be up to two or even three, they agreed. He was eleven by now and loved the work.

When Eduardo had left San Matías, the addition to the house had only the cement work done. There were no walls. The father said he would buy steel beams with the money Eduardo would be sending home. He needed people to help him with it. They had to be friends, as he had no money to pay for help now.

Eduardo mentioned that they should go home to help. It was a nice thought, except it didn't include directions on how to get money for the construction if nobody was working.

José remembers that they looked at the statue and wondered how the workers had been able to get up to the arm and put on the torch.

"They couldn't do it on our job," the brother remembers Eduardo saying.

"Doesn't anybody look at our job to make sure it is safe?" José asked.

"They say they do, but I never see nobody," Eduardo said. "The floor shakes."

José thought this was because no Mexicans worked on the Statue of Liberty. The ride home on the subway reinforced this idea. Anybody sitting near them left room so they wouldn't be rubbing up against these Mexicans.

Still, the thrill of seeing the statue made Eduardo call Silvia and tell her about it excitedly. She said she would have to come sometime. Eduardo and his brother sent the pictures to her and everybody in San Matías.

ALL VACANT LAND in New York, from marshes in Staten Island to abandoned junkyards in the Bronx, all these empty lots everywhere, covered with old tires, filthy refrigerators, and stained mattresses bloated by rain, is like a jewelry store window to a builder. Yet his is a slow dream. Possession of unoccupied land is not ruled by time of day or month of year. But when you get it, only a lottery is better.

The city has a series of rules that are designed to make the public feel it is being protected, and at times it actually is. Simultaneously, a land grab can appear honest and sometimes even be honest, while at all times it protects the politicians' right to accept bribes and the builders' right to bribe and cheat and steal while smiling for the public.

The system is the result of ages of politicians who proved that they were not nearly as stupid as they acted. They put together a system where many are paid and few are apprehended. It takes seven months to get permission to build anything in the city.

In Brooklyn, a number of empty lots on Middleton Street were in rem, which means the city and state have taken them over for nonpayment of taxes. An in rem procedure begins in the City Council, where a member lobbies for the return of the property to the one who lost it and has now paid the taxes. In Albany a member of the State Assembly proposes that with taxes paid, the property can be returned to the owner, who in this case received the tax money from Richie and then sold him the property.

The moment a person not in need of a lobotomy hears this antiquated, complicated, and thoroughly suspicious method being evoked, he must go on guard duty. As usual with in rem cases, the facts do not show, and therefore City Councilman Stanley Michels of the Washington Heights section of Manhattan grunted when he saw listed on the voting agenda of this day, "By Council Member Ward: SLR 471. Res. 3245. Assemblyman Genovesi. Reconveyance of block 2242 to Louis Ortiz."

"When this comes up, you abstain," he told two people sitting near him on the floor, new council members. "It's the things you don't vote for that save your life."

Michels had started doing this when he had two children in fine colleges and he preferred not to lose the means of keeping them there.

"What's the matter with it?" he was asked.

"The matter with it is I don't know what it is about. I don't know what any of these things are about. Neither do you. Let's keep investigations far away. Abstain."

At the end of the meeting they had the day's business, all resolutions and bills, together in one package on which the members started to vote.

"You vote yes on all except SLR 471, Resolution 3245," Michels said. "On that you abstain."

"And then?"

"And then you're all right. If it's got to do with buildings, then you're safe to abstain all the time."

SOMETIMES WHAT APPEARS to be a direct approach by a wounded citizen is made in the land business. The wounded citizen writes as one poor lone person, but when you parse the sentences you find lawyers, lobbyists, and references to phone call after phone call to city officials.

September 12, 1995
The Honorable Rudolph Giuliani
Mayor of the City of New York
New York, New York

Dear Mayor:

I am a registered Republican in the all Democratic neighborhood of Williamsburg, and have never asked for political help. I am deeply involved in community affairs, but I am not a politician!

It took us five years to change the zoning on Block 2240 in our neighborhood, from M1-2 to residential R-5. We own most of the lots in the block, but the City owns five parcels (see diagram attached herewith). Upon the recommendation of Borough President Howard Golden, we have been in contact with HPD regarding the acquisition of these lots. We would like to develop the City's lots in conjunction with our own residential construction on this block, so that the street should be uniformly developed. We are willing to sell or rent these lots for low-income people.

At this point in time, we already have approved plans and building

permits (copies attached) ready for our construction. We therefore
would need special assistance to obtain these permits from the City in a
timely fashion.

  We have been advised that you, the mayor, can make this happen.

Respectfully yours,
Eugene Ostreicher

There is no record of any return letter from Giuliani because if
it existed, it would have gone to Ostreicher and you would need a
crowbar to get it from him.

Immediately after this, a lawyer who knows the political land-
scape took over. Rosina Abramson has an honorable background as
counsel in the office of the old city council president, and her client
does not. It is obvious that a contractor trying it alone has as much
chance as he would trying to walk in the sky. For it can take the
work of the legitimate and illegitimate to get anything done.

Rosina Abramson, Esq.
135 East 57th Street
Suite 1100
New York, NY 10022

December 5, 1995
Phil Dameshek, Esq.
Dept. of General Services, Division of Real Estate
Municipal Building, 20th Floor So.
1 Centre Street

Dear Phil:

  Thank you for your advice regarding my client, Eugene Ostreicher,
who is seeking to redeem. . . . He has taken assignments from the former property owners. . . . I'm also enclosing a recent letter he wrote to
Mayor Giuliani. I would appreciate your guidance regarding how this
matter can be brought to Commissioner Diamond's attention. Thanks.

Dec. 7, 1995
Randal Fong, Assistant Commissioner, Planning
Dept. of General Services
Municipal Building, 20th Floor So.

Dear Randy:

I certainly understand your concerns regarding competition. I believe we can structure a restricted competition that protects and benefits all parties, particularly the City and the public. . . .

December 8, 1995
Richard J. Schwartz
Senior Advisor to the Mayor
City Hall

Dear Richard:

First, let me thank you for participating in the panel discussion on Business Improvement Districts, sponsored by the Municipal Affairs committee of the Bar Association. Your focus on encouraging private enterprise inspired me to think more creatively regarding an interest in a client which should coincide with furthering city policies, both with regard to in rem vacant land and affordable housing. . . .

December 12, 1995
Hon. William J. Diamond
Commissioner, Dept. of General Services
Municipal Building, 17th Floor
1 Centre Street

Re: Privatizing in rem vacant land, fostering private development—
   a pilot project proposal

Dear Commissioner Diamond:

. . . I understand that DGS has recently suspended its Adjacent Home Owners Program (AHOP). . . . Rather than eliminate this privatization strategy, I suggest eliminating restrictions and expanding the program, at least on a pilot basis. . . .

A case in point . . . is presented by the situation in which my client,

Eugene Ostreicher, finds himself. Mr. Ostreicher, through his own personal initiative and individual enterprise, has begun to turn an abandoned block in Williamsburg into affordable housing. My client is seeking to redeem in rem properties adjacent to property he is developing on Lorimer and Middleton Streets . . . in the Williamsburg section of Brooklyn. I'm enclosing a recent letter he wrote to Mayor Giuliani expressing his desire to build on the in rem parcels. . . .

Sincerely yours,
Rosina Abramson

CHAPTER SEVENTEEN

I t happened in the morning, and whoever the workers were—Polish from up in Greenpoint, Mexican from Brighton and Sunset Park—they had already gone to the hospital. The fire and police vehicles had pulled out by the time Charles Blaich, a deputy chief of the Fire Department, arrived in a department station wagon. He looked at the construction site as if it were an empty casket. This building job on Lorimer Street was a block of four-story multiple dwellings that the builder stated was to house faculty for Hasidic schools. The first wall on Lorimer Street was a stack of cinder blocks without enough support to stop the wind. Which is not a turned phrase but a precise estimate of the wall's strength: On this February morning at 7:30 in 1996 a wind strong enough to make people pull their coats around themselves came along Lorimer Street, and it simply knocked the wall down.

They had poured concrete and put heavy cinder blocks on the floor. How did they expect that to hold up? Blaich looked at the twisted beams that were the result.

As Blaich looked at the wreckage, Richie Ostreicher showed up. "Those idiots," he said.

Richie Schairer, liaison between police and the Hasidic community, arrived, took a look, and left. "Be back," he said.

Blaich called in John Humble, the trade representative for the American Iron and Steel Institute. Blaich knew him from courses in construction he had taken over a period of twenty years. The steel being used in the buildings here on Lorimer Street was dirt cheap compared to wood, but it still had great strength. That was Humble's opinion until he saw gaps in the building walls.

"What if there had been a fire?" Humble said.

Blaich stiffened. There had been a fire-alarm fire in Bay Ridge, and the C-joists had collapsed with no warning. Later inspection showed they had the appearance of cooked spaghetti.

After this, out of sight and sound in the Bronx, two units of firefighters were working a four-alarm in a building where C-joists were put up for installation on a new story being erected over the original buildings. The C-joists had no fire protection, and touched by flame, they failed immediately and soundlessly. They too were reduced to cooked spaghetti.

Collapses of C-joists became common in the parts of Williamsburg where Ostreicher built.

C-joists are cold-formed steel and were first used in 1973 to rebuild at least some of Bushwick, a neighborhood that, for the most part, was turned into char by arson in the '60s and '70s. Fires had been set for insurance by owners of buildings that were empty when whites fled the arrival of people of color. The fires then were set without the excuse of money.

C-joists are long silver beams that can be from six to twelve inches wide and an inch and a half thick. They come with an open side, thus forming the C, and the joist is then fitted onto tracks of a floor beam or wall beam. There should be sixteen inches between each C-joist. The C-joists can cost as little as a few dollars apiece but can go as high as $20. For builders cutting corners, the less you use, the more money sticks to the pocket, rather than the supplier's bill. The C-joists barely resist the first lick of a fire and become sudden death. To guard against this, contractors supposedly cover the deck C-joists with a concrete spray and the ones on the wall with plasterboard.

Blaich and Humble looked at the basement. The block of Lorimer Street buildings was supposed to have elevators, but instead there were wood staircases to the cellar. Blaich took a look from one end of the cellar to the other. A fire could come through here like it was a wind tunnel.

A firefighter coming into a burning building can gauge how long it will take burning wood beams to give way. It could be five minutes, it could be nine. Experience tells him when to flee. But when the C-joists get ready to give, you have nothing to see and everything to fear.

FIRE DEPARTMENT
2/9/96

1. e-239 responded to reported bldg collapse 49 Lorimer St. Upon arrival found row of new construction in progress. Bldgs are 2-story M/D's.
2. Questionable construction tactics being used. Bldg's experienced a lean-to collapse in early phase of construction.
3. Request review of bldg. dept. permits and architectural plans.
4. Request on site inspection by Building Dept.

Respectfully submitted,
Joseph M. Sweeney Lt. E-230

TO: Edmund P. Cunningham, Chief of Fire Prev.
FROM: Roderick J. O'Connor, Battalion Chief, Bn. 57

Upon receiving the report from E-230 and speaking with Capt. Regan E-230, I performed an on-site inspection. I concur with Lt. Sweeney's opinion and request for an immediate inspection by the building department.

The materials used for this construction appear to be acceptable but the practices putting them to use does not seem appropriate. There have been two incidents of collapse and upon viewing the site today, the floors in place seem uneven and incapable of withstanding the heavy loads they will be expected to carry. I collected two pieces of the metal floor beams used. It seems that if the flooring material (three quarters inch plywood) is not placed on these floor beams immediately, the metal floor beams tend to twist loose from their perch which is a cutout in the concrete block walls.

This construction site should be inspected as soon as possible in order to prevent any possible improper practices of construction. It is open frame now and can easily be evaluated.

Respectfully submitted,
Roderick O'Connor

ON FEBRUARY 29, 1996, there was a third collapse, this one in the dark of night. The sound ran down empty streets. At that hour, with no workers on the job, nobody was hurt. At daylight, Chief Dillon of the Fifth Battalion arrived from the firehouse on Union Avenue, alongside the Ninetieth Precinct. Around a corner of the building was Truck Eight of Police Emergency Services. They were not needed—this time.

Dillon arrived at the scene of new rubble and had his men put up yellow crime scene tape. The Mexican workers stood across the street, uncertain. Suddenly Richie Ostreicher got out of a car with police lights and shields and any other placard he had been able to get from police commanders who thought they were dealing with a police chaplain. He called to the laborers, "We go to work."

Dillon said no.

"Forget it," Ostreicher told his crew. "We go to work."

Dillon said, "You don't."

"Who are you?" Ostreicher said.

"I'm Chief Dillon, New York City Fire Department. I closed this place."

"You can't do that."

"Yes, I can. I'm in charge here until I hand over the place to somebody else, the Buildings Department."

"I own this place," Ostreicher said.

"I closed it," Dillon said.

"What do you know?" he asked Dillon.

"I know I'm a fire chief in charge."

"You don't know buildings."

"I went to school for it," Dillon said.

"What degree did you get?"

"GED." (Everybody knew that he got that degree from a high school continuation course.)

"What's that?"

"General Engineering Diploma."

"Oh," Richie Ostreicher said.

Dillon's men stood in a semicircle with him and tried not to smile.

Now Ostreicher said, "Can I talk to you?"

"That's what you're doing," Dillon said.

"No, I mean, alone. Over there." He pointed to the other side of the street.

"All right," Dillon said. He tapped his aide, Chris Steidinger, who walked over with him.

"We can talk alone," Ostreicher said.

"We are alone. He counts as me," Dillon said.

Ostreicher went into his pocket and brought out a gold badge. He had it cupped in his hand and held the hand close to his pants pocket.

"Do you know what this is?"

Dillon looked at. A gold shield with two stars on it. Some kind of police inspector's badge.

Dillon said nothing.

"This doesn't mean anything to you?" Ostreicher said, pushing the cupped hand toward Dillon.

"Are you a member of the Police Department of the City of New York?" Dillon said.

Quickly Ostreicher put the badge back in his pocket. Once Dillon started making it official, he stepped back.

Dillon drove back to the firehouse.

FIRE DEPARTMENT
ENGINE CO. 230
FEB. 25, 1996

Responded to a structural collapse at 49 Lorimer Street. This was the THIRD COLLAPSE in the past few weeks at this construction site. Fortunately, the workmen were able to escape without injury. The Owner Chaim Ostreicher was given three summons.

I AM REQUESTING A PERMANENT STOP WORK ORDER AND JOINT INSPECTION OF CONSTRUCTION SITE TO DETERMINE STRUCTURAL STABILITY OF EXISTING STRUCTURES.

See attached report dated 2/9/96 from BC O'Connor, fwded after the SECOND COLLAPSE. . . .

Respectfully submitted,
Edward J. Regan, Captain, E230.

Hertzberg & Sanchez
Consulting Engineers
295 Northern Boulevard, Great Neck, NY 11921-4701

Feb. 26, 1996
Department of Buildings, Borough of Brooklyn
Att: Mr. Darryl Hilton
Chief Inspector

RE: 29 Lorimer Street (#300437800)
21 Lorimer Street (#300437837)
41 Lorimer Street (#300437064)

Dear Mr. Hilton:
This will confirm that Hertzberg and Sanchez will be observing the

construction in progress to assure that the walls will be properly braced by the installation of the floor joists.

The bricklayers have been instructed to brace the walls before they close for the day.

We require immediate approval to continue with the work as vandalism is rampant in the area.

Very truly yours,
Louis Sanchez, P.E.
Vice-President

The engineers wrote as if they were in charge, which they were. Because the city Building Department, which sounds like a massive government bureau, is so small, with only eight hundred workers, including office maintenance workers, receptionists, and computer workers, there is no way to inspect the eight hundred thousand buildings in the city, particularly if City Hall cuts the funds to nothing. Buildings Department people rarely see any structures. The architects and professional engineers supposedly put up their reputations and license and certify each of their construction jobs. If anything falls down, their licenses flop with it. That never happens. What does happen every day is that the trust of a huge city is given to people with no official responsibility.

On March 14, 1996, Michael Caterina, a compliance officer from the Occupational Safety and Health Administration—which is commonly known as OSHA—received an anonymous complaint about collapses of Ostreicher buildings on Lorimer Street. In the building world, an anonymous complaint is too often a phoned-in stiletto. Business competitors or personal enemies regard them as a marvelous way to hurt another. Caterina, then, was wary when he walked down Lorimer Street.

Here, standing in the street, a statue of a biblical character who suddenly was breathing, was Eugene Ostreicher. He was short, stocky, and suspicious. He was in black from hat to shoes. A great white beard billowed at the cheeks. Prominent dark eyebrows stood out over his pale blue eyes. He had the brusque movements of someone used to being in charge on the street. He was impatient when Michael Caterina of OSHA spoke to him in the middle of Lorimer.

Caterina asked Ostreicher if there had ever been a collapse at the site.

"What collapse? What are you talking about? Do you see a collapse? Tell me. Do you see a collapse?" He waved at his site of attached three-story brick condominiums. "A collapse. Where did you get that from?"

"I heard that," Caterina said.

"Where did you hear that from? Who told you that? You heard a fairy tale from somebody."

"You're stating that there have been no collapses at this site?" Caterina said in official tones.

"Absolutely. There never is a collapse here."

Caterina went back to the OSHA offices on Varick Street in Manhattan and typed up a report with Ostreicher's answer to an official question from a government agent.

If Ostreicher hadn't been so quick and boisterous to hurl out his denials, Caterina might have helped him. OSHA has only civil penalties, and the staff would have been anxious to push Ostreicher away from dangerous practices. He liked loud lying better. And this became obvious, and started Caterina on investigating the building being done on the block. First, there were witnesses who had seen a collapse. Then there were the Fire Department records. Caterina then began to talk about this lying with James Vanderberg, a thirty-two-year-old agent for the United States Department of Labor. This agency could prosecute criminally. The file on Ostreicher now included the results of all this investigating, along with Fire Department reports of collapses on the scene and of Ostreicher's involvement with the buildings. Neither memos nor Fire Department reports would go away. They were written and filed in the time of computers, but the

paper lasted and the reports retained their clarity and impact about
the three collapses in February 1996.

JOSEPH TRIVISONNO, the buildings superintendent for Brooklyn,
was in anguish trying to keep his job against stiff interference on the
Lorimer Street buildings. Suddenly, Trivisonno was bewildered by the
papers about a building being built at 26 Heyward Street, up the block
from the brick condominiums being built by Eugene Ostreicher. The
more he looked at the papers, the more his eyes narrowed. He was
on crazy street. The plans for 26 Heyward were for a building that
was 108 feet deep. That allowed room for the building and for a
35-foot-deep backyard as required by law. Trivisonno knew that the
lot was only 100 feet deep. Somewhere the builder had to reach into
the air and come up with eight feet of Brooklyn land. The owner of
the land behind the offending building said he wanted to keep his
eight feet and would fight all the way to the Supreme Court for it.

At the end of 1996, two businessmen who were of the Puppa
sect of Hasidim bought 26 Heyward and wanted to change the footprint of the building, the floor-to-area ratio, to build nine condominiums in the five-story building to house faculty for a yeshiva.
Under the zoning laws, if you put even as little as a rabbi's office in a
building, you were allowed to enlarge it. Excavation for number 26,
on an empty lot next door to number 18, and the placement of struts
between the old and new buildings (which meant the new building
was holding up the old one) put cosmetic cracks in the old building.
A complaint came in by phone, and Trivisonno had his inspectors
stop the job until 18 Heyward was stabilized. No blueprints had been
turned in. Another call brought a claim that there was no such religious anchor as a rabbi's office in their five-story building, but there
were condominiums that would go for $350,000 each.

The records of the United States Department of Education show
that a great college was located in the tan two-story building a few
doors up at 105 Heyward Street. Supposedly, it was a converted

yeshiva grammar school. It became the most ambitious temporal reach of the Skver Hasidic group, who came out of Russian mud to Williamsburg. They also occupy their own town of New Square, in near upstate Rockland County.

In a bakery on the corner of Heyward, the milk bottles have the labels of New Square Farms, the upstate milk farm of the Skver group. There are about three thousand living in New Square, eleven hundred of them registered voters. All are dedicated to study and the passing of knowledge and wisdom to those who follow. While this is a beautiful way of life, all this studying takes as many as thirteen hours a day, and this leaves no time for a job. Simultaneously, bills must be paid with more than prayer. One day, four of the men of the village sat down and developed a plan that would allow the village to study and still have an income. They announced a university-level school called Toldos Yakov Yosef. The students were not required to attend classes, but regular contact with an assigned mentor was supposedly required. The school was beautiful to run in that it required no start-up fees other than the few dollars for applications for government Pell grants for students. The Pell grants are American government at its most indescribably beautiful. Named after Claiborne Pell, the senator from Rhode Island, they are federal college tuition assistance grants—not loans—awarded to undergraduates and based on income. It gives a student without enough money some help to finish an education. The students receive grants of $1,500 or so, with a maximum of $3,300 a year. The program has some defenses against the stray schemer, but it never envisioned nor threw up breastworks against an organized criminal raid from a place like Heyward Street, Williamsburg. Soon, the new university had 1,544 checks for Pell grants coming in the mail to the school. This made the school more than somewhat profitable. . . .

Because there was no school.

While 105 Heyward grammar school was the address, there were no students. There was no faculty. There were no books.

On streets whose waking hours were dedicated to trimming corners, Eugene Ostreicher looked up from his cinder blocks and bricks
a block or so away, and found his shaky buildings produced loud,
treacherous candy store money in comparison to 105 Heyward, where
they had only to empty the mailbox each day to gain their fortune.

They collected the Pell grants for the first year of their no-show
college. There wasn't even a letter asking a question. They went on
to the second year and it was better yet: they added a few students
and received grants for them. After this, year after year it went on,
and the school brought in $40 million of government money. All of
New Square studied and prayed, and the bills were paid. Four people
ran the school. They spent all of their time cashing checks and evad-
ing inspections.

A federal Department of Education group, including agent Brian
Hickey, finally moved on Heyward Street, the home of the great
university. This time, Hickey came in with a scheduled government
inspection, from which there could be neither postponement nor
subterfuge. Also, it was scheduled for five days, from the second
through the sixth of June, 1992, with a full team of inspectors. The
school could not stand the light of a heavy candle.

The inspectors began with the book lists of the college students.
They discovered that books bought with Pell grants were high school
books for the eleventh and twelfth grades of the yeshiva schools
upstate in New Square.

The inspectors found that the chief administrators listed on the
Pell grant records were: Chancellor Chaim Berger, the "brilliant thirty-
two-year-old nationally known educator," and the registrar, Kalmen
Stern.

Hickey found the chancellor in a room on the first floor. He
was in fact a ninety-one-year-old man.

"Hello," Berger said.

"Are you the chancellor?" he was asked.

"Hello," the old man said.

Next Hickey met the registrar, Kalmen Stern. Somehow he got Stern to write something for him. "Write down what you think of your job," Hickey said. Stern wrote, "He has a good car." Then he wrote what he thought of America: "A-M-R-I-C-A."

The first floor of 105 Heyward had some old men reading religious textbooks. They had been gathered up from the neighborhood and thrown into a sudden university.

There was a great amount of noise from the second floor, where the student body, preschool and kindergarten kids ages three to six, was running about. They had been dispossessed from their usual first-floor playroom to make room for the university inspection.

The inspection team asked to speak to six college students. The school could produce only four. Registrar Stern presented a man who said he was a college student.

"When did you enroll?" Hickey asked.

"What do you mean by enroll?" the man asked.

A woman had a transcript that showed two years of philosophy courses.

An agent asked her, "Do you know what philosophy is?"

"No."

A woman named Polyna was introduced as an English major. She needed a Russian interpreter to speak to one of the inspectors.

"Student number 21," the federal report stated, "could not recall when he started at the school, but thought he had attended last year. Student 21 stated that he did not understand most of what went on because he doesn't know the English language.

"Student No. 23 stated he did not have time to discuss education. Student 23 did not respond to questions regarding the subjects studied. He asked the reviewers to put the questions in writing and send them to him."

When the reviewers were leaving, the educational genius, ninety-one-year-old Chaim Berger, looked up from a nap.

"Hello."

Back in the Manhattan offices, the federal education team filed a simple report: "We are requesting emergency action and termination be taken against Toldos Yakov Yosef."

The students and school were an illusion, but the money from government grants was more than somewhat real.

The New Square educators took down $40 million from the government over ten years. In recorded American crime—groups under five members, no weapons—this receives all-time honorable mention.

But then it went further. There were four people sent to prison over this. On the day they went in, Skvers were writing letters to get them out. The Skvers were ceaseless and went from one official to the other until, in the year 2000, they wound up with a president's wife who thought everything she looked at, from trinket to mansion, was hers. Hillary Clinton was running for the Senate. All Hasidic groups voted against her, for good reason: She was a woman. However, at New Square, she willingly walked on the women's side of the street, and did not shake hands with the men. When meeting the wise man, Rebbe Twersky, she sat with the desk between them. The town of New Square alone voted for her, by 1,200 to nothing. After the election, all she saw was black hats. She then made an appointment at the White House for Rebbe Twersky. The date was for a Friday. The rebbe and his people were unsure of where the White House was. One of them called an editor of a Jewish publication in Brooklyn and asked, "Can the rebbe go to Washington and come back in time for sundown?" At the White House, Twersky and Ms. Clinton, now a senator-elect, sat happily as Bill Clinton issued a presidential pardon for the New Square prisoners. That night in Borough Park, Brooklyn, a non-Jew, and therefore one who could answer a phone that day, rushed into a synagogue and told the son of one of the New Square prisoners, "They pardoned your father!"

IN FEBRUARY 1997, the mayor was up for reelection, and with the first rustle of campaign money sounding in Williamsburg, the expediter for 26 Heyward Street headed out of the computer room and went down the hall into Joseph Trivisonno's office. Trivisonno remembers the expediter telling him to get a zoning change that would take care of the missing eight feet. Trivisonno said his department did not get zoning changes or grab land out of thin air. Trivisonno says the expediter said to him, "You get approval for us."

Trivisonno remembers saying that he could not.

"We'll get you."

"The next thing was somebody saying I was anti-Semitic," Trivisonno said.

Kenny Fisher, a city councilman from an old, well-known Brooklyn political family, suppressed that quickly.

Afterward Trivisonno felt the first fatigue. "If I had to ask for all this help for nothing, then how am I going to last through something that actually happens?" he said to a friend.

MAYOR GIULIANI ANNOUNCED a policy of closing X-rated movie houses and bookstores because they hurt children. He ordered seventy-five building inspectors out to do the work. Forty percent of a store had to be legitimate books and videos. The rest of it could be for adults. As the history of censorship could serve as wallpaper for a psychiatric ward, sex shop owners began to stock shelves with biographies of Daniel Boone. Once these hit the required 40 percent, here came all those adult books.

This brought the former Carmella Lauretano, who is the wife of a building inspector on detached duty in sex shops, to see Trivisonno. As Trivisonno recalls it, she said to him, "Make my husband get off that job. My husband is a building inspector. You have him in whorehouses. My husband is a family man. You got to stop this."

FIRE CHIEF BLAICH called a meeting of technical people from the Buildings Department, engineers and experts in construction. They stood on the street in front of the Lorimer Street buildings, and each time Blaich pointed out a dangerous flaw, they all concurred. "Ostreicher should be stopped from doing any building," Blaich said. "We'll put it in writing. We'll all sign it and that should put it over." Suddenly the group with him began to shrink. "You better do that yourself," one of them said. Blaich said, "Why only me?" The guy said, "Because you're civil service."

Blaich wrote the letter and sent it in.

The answer came on August 26, 1998, when the first of eleven certificates of occupancy was signed by Joseph Trivisonno and issued to the owner of the Lorimer Street buildings. A certificate of occupancy means you can move into, rent, or sell the building, which has been certified as legal by the City of New York.

Trivisonno said that the building defects had been cured and that in all other cases such as this the building was allowed to be completed and certificates issued.

Blaich shrugged. He had gone further than anybody had before. He had made charges on paper and signed it. The cave-in this time was Trivisonno. Of course it wasn't enough. Nothing helped Trivisonno, either. In City Hall, they still complained that Trivisonno was obstructing commerce in Brooklyn. Commissioner Gaston Silva wanted him to take a leave. "Teitelbaum is the one who wants to get you," Silva said, "but we hear he may be going. He'll head Giuliani's campaign when he runs for the Senate. When he goes, you can come right back."

Next, Silva asked about the problem with 26 Heyward Street. Trivisonno said the owner had claimed faculty housing that in fact wouldn't be there, and that there was an eight-foot overlap problem. Silva hung up. Trivisonno now heard from a secretary: "They want you out." Trivisonno called the commissioner and asked who wanted him out. Trivisonno resigned in March. He was replaced by Tarek Zeid, whose wife is an expediter. Zeid departed and soon, Commissioner Silva was gone.

CHAPTER EIGHTEEN

That day, Eduardo got home by 4:30 and called Silvia, and this time he got her before she left for work. She had spent most of the hours after finishing her morning job at the mall on the other side of Highway 6. She had bought pants and blouses for her sisters back home and Winnie the Pooh toys for her nieces. Her sister Emilia was with her now; she had been stopped twice at the border and frightened several times in the desert, but there was no thought of giving up. Silvia got her jobs at both the barbecue restaurant and the Olive Garden. Between them they were sending home $2,500 a month. They now had a one-bedroom apartment, near where Silvia had first lived. That one had been filled with enough relatives to form the trunk of a family tree.

When Eduardo called Silvia this time, he talked about his job. "He told me he had to climb up on the building," Silvia remembers. "He told me that the work was very hard. Then he said again that he had to climb up on the building. He said the sun was cruel. He had to climb up. He said he didn't like that. It seemed shaky to him. I knew he had never been that high up. I asked him if it was dangerous, and he said it was. I didn't know what else to say. He was there. I was here. What could we do?"

For Eduardo the days had changed only because he was not staying home in the room so much. Now he came to the room in Brighton Beach right after work, took a shower, and went out. He was the youngest of the group by five years, and the age difference with the roommates had become wearing. On Friday night, the others started out at the round table in the kitchen, and Alejandro drank one beer with great gulps, then another and a third, after which he reached for the bottle of tequila. The rest tried to keep up with him. Originally when they did this, Eduardo would sit on the kitchen floor and make fun of them, or he'd go into their room and fall asleep. But over the months he saw that drinking was a morose celebration and that conversation consisted of short bursts of despair. When they needed more alcohol, somebody went down to the store on Neptune Avenue. Later, Eduardo noticed that one of them would leave and wouldn't return for some time, after which a couple of others would leave. After a few months, he figured out they were going with prostitutes in doorways and cars. Once, in one long drunk that went on for a day and a half, Alejandro drank thirty bottles of Corona beer and a bottle of tequila. There were no classic drinking stories told of this episode. Only the number of bottles was cited. Alejandro had a fierce hangover, but neither he nor the others could speak about it with any humor. One sad night of drink in the kitchen became another the next week, and the weeks became months and the months would become years.

Not only did late-night homesickness torture them, but the loneliness became more searing in the sunlight. They sat in the room and told themselves—and then their wives and children on the phone—that they would be home soon. They did not learn English because they were sure of leaving for home forever. They drank at sunrise on weekends and spoke only in Spanish, thus robbing themselves of any chance for better work.

Many times, Eduardo went to watch television in his friend Lucino's room two flights over Kings Highway, a subway stop up from Brighton. Lucino lived with his cousin Julisa and her husband and two children. He was a short, stocky, handsome thirty-two-year-old with a prominent nose. Working in Mexico City as an accountant, he saw there was no future and left. He came unannounced to Julisa's apartment. Why wouldn't he? He was a relative. After a couple of days, it was plain. Why would he ever leave? He lived there.

Following this, one night Lucino's brother Pedro called. "I'm here," he said.

"Where?" Julisa said.

"At the airport. I'm coming over."

Pedro came in, sat down, weary from travel, and went to sleep. Next, a cousin, José, called from the airport. He, too, was coming over. He, too, could not be moved if you put dynamite under his feet. Soon another of Lucino's brothers called from the airport. Julisa couldn't remember his name, but knew he could eat. Lucino mentioned vaguely that Aunt Matilda might be coming in from Mexico. Julisa thought that this would be sometime in the distant future, and in the meantime Aunt Matilda could get arrested at the border. Two nights later, the phone rang. "I'm here!" Aunt Matilda cried.

First they put the men in one room and the women and baby in the other. Finally, Julisa's husband told her that her cousin had to clear the place. Lucino did. He told all the others to leave, and he took over a room for himself. Lucino was out looking for work from the start. He knew one here and another there and he wound up catching on with a construction job that was starting on Middleton Street. He worked there with Eduardo. Lucino had a treasure: a room to himself. Soon Eduardo was walking into the apartment with his head hanging like a penitent's and he'd slip into Lucino's room without talking. They usually drank and watched pro basketball. When he went in there on one night, Julisa heard something slapping a board and one of them laughing. They were playing some board game, soccer football probably.

JULISA WAS NINETEEN and in the second year of medical school in Mexico City when she and a couple of students came for a holiday to her hometown of San José edo de Tlaxcala, which is near Puebla. She had a twin sister, Lourdes, and seven brothers.

Julisa and her classmates arrived on the one day of the year that the fair came to town. Her glance took in children's rides and the booths for games and stopped when she saw the handsome young guy in the booth with soccer games on the counter. The guy was putting prizes on a shelf. Of course the woman is not supposed to be so forward as to walk up alone to a booth with a man behind it.

No such thing could happen. The young man in the booth, José J. Eduardo, had his entire attention captured by Julisa, whose long hair and large beautiful eyes filled with gladness caused her dignity to evaporate. His mother, who sold lottery tickets a few booths away, thought she noticed something. He came out from behind the counter and promptly stumbled. He then ran up to Julisa and the others and asked if they wanted to play the soccer game on the table outside the booth. Julisa answered for everybody. She said yes and she went up to that strange game and played it as best she could, and played it for most of the night, her smile so expressive, her shoulders moving with her words, and all of it for this young man who was handsome and so attentive.

He could not wait to graze her.

She decided to marry him.

Professors at the medical school in Mexico City said dolefully that she wouldn't be able to finish school if she was married.

"When you fall in love, whatever you say, I still get married," she says. But she stayed in school, although she was studying with one emotion and dying to get married with another.

Two years later, she came to her town to get married in church. The reception was in her home.

She was pregnant in five minutes and was angry with herself and her husband. The couple didn't have enough money, and their families couldn't help. She took a bookkeeping job in a Mexico City bakery. The new husband studied chemical engineering but still had to travel with his family to these one-day fairs. With her last year in school and three years of residency in front of her, Julisa had a miscarriage. She couldn't even pay for books. She dropped out. I'll try next year, she told herself.

Her twin sister, Lourdes, and her husband went with another couple to Tijuana, and Lourdes called to report that they were going across the border on Saturday night. The hospital in Tijuana called on Sunday to say that Lourdes and two others were dead as a result of beatings that were apparently handed out by marauding thieves in the scrub. Julisa had been raised in the same womb and bed with her sister, but she shucked off as much misery as possible and tried to help raise the money to bring Lourdes back for a funeral.

Two years later, she and her husband were living in defeat in Mexico City. She wasn't a day closer to returning to school, and he couldn't get a job in engineering. They saved and borrowed $1,800 for a coyote to cross them at Tijuana. We will make it all up in America, and I'll come back for school, she told herself. Then she and the husband left for Tijuana.

Fear owned her as she walked and ran over the same soil where her sister had died. The coyote had them hide in a garbage dump. Then they were among a group of five who stuffed themselves into the back of a van going to Los Angeles.

The woman who rented them the first room in Brooklyn instructed Julisa and her husband never to go outside except to go to work and back, because the police would arrest them, and the police were everywhere.

Julisa brought two babies home to these rooms but learned only snatches of English. "We were afraid to go to school at night for English," she remembers. They moved into the rooms on Kings Highway, and her brother Valentine came to live with them, which gave them an extra hand with baby-sitting and the rent. Mostly, the husband watched the babies while she went out and cleaned houses. When she came home, he left to sweep out a beauty parlor. She paid out the toughest thousand dollars for a booklet, "Fast Practical English," put out by the UCEDA English Institute, which counted her thousand in English. She picked up a couple of new words and not much more after listening to the CD sent by the institute. Supposedly, there were classes she could attend in a hall someplace, but she was never able to get there.

While a social worker was complaining about the UCEDA English Institute to Joel Magallan, SJ, the director of the Asociación Tepeyac de New York, he waved a hand.

"The Mexicans already know a second language," he said. "The ones from Puebla were raised on Aztec Indian—we call it Nahuatl. Then in school they had to learn mainstream Spanish. The other Indian language they learn as babies is Tarahumara. That is spoken in the Sierra Nevada mountains. Otomi is the first language of those in Baja. Mayan is spoken first in Chiapas."

One day, Julisa's brother left on his bicycle for his job at a refrigerator manufacturer on Atlantic Avenue, a wide, extremely busy street. A while later, a policeman came to the door to tell Julisa that her brother was dead. There had been a two-car accident, and he couldn't get out of the way and was killed.

Once more, she had to grope through her grief to come up with money for a dead body.

Now here she is, five years after leaving medical school, standing in her room, a baby sleeping on her bed that is covered with a big brilliant red Mexican blanket. Still, energy and enthusiasm fill her eyes and brighten her face and she says that soon, yes, soon, she will be able to leave this place and go back to medical school in Mexico. It is still the reason she does not try to find time to go to school for English. Why should she? She just told you that soon she would be going back.

Never once does she pause to realize that she has no money for any school, and that she is a cleaning woman when she should be a doctor, and that her husband is sweeping up in a beauty parlor when he should be an engineer. And that all around them the lives of the Mexicans are the same. Here in her house right now, Lucino is an accountant, and he was the cheapest of labor. Visiting for the basketball games was Alejandro, an upholsterer who works for perhaps a dollar over minimum wage. Simultaneously you'd look at each week's pay with Mexican peasant eyes—it was rich man's money—and then add their weekly bills in Brooklyn and realize they live at the bottom.

At those moments when Julisa suddenly saw the walls of her room for what they were, a life sentence, she said to herself right away, soon I will go back to school. She says that through each year.

Does she still love the husband she met at the fair?

"For my children I love him."

And Eduardo worked at bricklaying, which he knew, for the lowest money in all of construction. He didn't have the slightest idea that a white in New York gets $23 an hour for the same work. How could he know such a thing? Nobody could speak English, and the only people they knew had jobs as bad or worse. Sometimes Julisa felt sad for Eduardo when he walked past her as if afraid to talk.

When Eduardo went out at other times, he hung out in front of the Mexican store on Neptune Avenue with a kid named El Viejo, which means "the old man." He was twenty. They went to the boardwalk at Coney Island and played video games and talked with others who were their age. Frequently, they now rode the el up to Fifth Avenue in Brooklyn, where one night in a Mexican restaurant the waitress looked at Eduardo and when he put his chin down, she put her hand under it and lifted it. "I like you the best," she told him. His chin went right back down.

When they left the place, everybody was laughing at Eduardo because of his shyness. It was one thing for the older guys back in the room to make fun of him, but these were kids his own age. He told them that he would show them all. He would go back to the restaurant and take the waitress out of there for all to see how much she loved him. A week later, he walked ahead of the others into the restaurant; he didn't know exactly what he was going to do, but for sure they were not going to laugh at him anymore because he was going to talk to that waitress and make her like him and go out with him. Nobody would laugh. He walked in and found another waitress working. He asked for the one he wanted. "She quit," the owner said.

ON MARCH 11, 1999, an application for a $2 million general liability insurance policy on Ostreicher property under the name of Faye Industries Corp., 527 Bedford Avenue, was forwarded by a broker to Greg Portnoy, a broker in the Westchester suburb of White Plains who places accounts with the First Financial Insurance Company, which has an Illinois license but conducts business all over, much of it in the state of North Carolina.

The application called for the policy to be in effect on March 17, 1999. It was a simple three-page questionnaire of yes-or-no answers in boxes. There were two questions about background, the first of which appears to be there only to please the religious beliefs of Carolina:

> 7. Any past losses or claims relating to sexual abuse or molestation allegations, discrimination or negligent hiring?

Let no hands commit a sin of the flesh in a lumberyard. (The discrimination and hiring can be considered a throw-in.)

Answer: no.

The next question was at the center of the insurance business:

8. During the past ten years has any applicant been convicted
of any degree of the crime of arson? The question must be
answered by any applicant. Failure to disclose the substance of an arson conviction is a misdemeanor punishable
by a sentence of up to one year of imprisonment.

Answer: no.

There is not even a thought of punishment, save loss of this
particular policy, for some grubby child molester. Strike one match
without admitting it and, according to the piece of paper, leg irons
can be clamped on.

As collateral, Faye Industries listed ten vacant lots and two
buildings. The lots happened to have buildings on them. Industrial
Enterprises listed five vacant lots and one building. Ramon, Inc.,
listed four empty lots and a building. Both Ostreichers said they had
three empty lots. A cousin, Samuel Newman, was down for three
vacant lots. Middleton Street, where everybody worked, had seven
addresses that were listed as vacant lots. This could disorient an
experienced postman. Later, a lawyer for First Financial thought that
the number of addresses for Middleton Street were there to dizzify
those looking at the application.

Then on the third page of the application there were three
questions, short and easily answered.

12. Any structural alterations contemplated?

Answer: no.

13. Any demolition exposure contemplated?

Answer: no.

14. Has applicant been active in or is currently active in joint
ventures?

Answer: no.

One possible explanation for all of Ostreicher's answers was
that it was cheaper to insure an empty lot than a building full of

workers. Anyway, who was going to check? If there was no catastrophe, the policy would sleep in a file. Who would be dumb enough to list all the work being done and pay those higher premiums?

On the last blank on the application, Ostreicher came up with his personal safety net:

APPLICANT'S SIGNATURE: _____

The space was blank.

Two brokers and an insurance company collected premiums. Therefore, the policy was good. What does it matter if the guy forgot to sign his name? Just an oversight. We'll get it when we get it.

They could not envision Ostreicher sitting at a legal proceeding and saying, in substance, "It is not my policy. I never signed it. This policy is full of mistakes made by some clerk in the insurance company. I have never seen such an application full of errors. You can see I never signed it. Where is my signature?"

8/10/99 BF 25 FIRE OPERATION REPORT
58 Middleton Street. On arrival found cause for alarm to be a partial collapse of a building under construction with workers trapped. Engine 269 stretched hand lines, stood fast assisted with first aid and victim transport. Three non-life-threatening injuries to workers, all taken to Bellevue. A two story building 20 feet by 40 feet. A phone alarm at 11:17 units here four minutes later 11:21 all hands at 11:23 three engines and two trucks and special units rescue two squad one. Under control 12:42. Three civilian victims. Chief Corcoran from 11th division pd 90. Buildings Mr. Maniscalco on site. Supervisor Leon Schwimmer Industrial, 527 Bedford. Block Foreman Colin Torney.

Since the accident had happened at the far end of the construction site, none of the Mexicans knew about it. Only that something had happened.

The three workers battered in the collapse of a floor went out through the building's rear and were taken over the bridge to Bellevue Hospital on First Avenue in Manhattan, which is the Yankee Stadium of emergency rooms. Their names on police aided cards were Herb Lubin, Brian Dubois, and Robert Jackson. All the Mexican workers were at the other end of the construction site. They let these three work together because they spoke no Spanish. The injuries were minor: a sprain, a bruise. They had no medical coverage from the job. They walked out of Bellevue and went into the perpetual night of itinerant workers.

Only Eduardo and his brother José knew about this collapse. A few days later, the boss, Leo Schwimmer, sent them up to the building. (Leon Schwimmer, known as Leo, is the father-in-law of Faye Schwimmer, who is the daughter of Eugene Ostreicher. Faye and her husband, Ed, who live in Ostreicher's house at 527 Bedford, are part owners of the sites on Lorimer and Middleton Streets. Including the founding father, Eugene, there are eight Ostreicher relatives on the building company's payroll.) José says now, "The building wasn't level. It didn't have a lot of beams. We wanted to know who was working there but we couldn't ask or we'd be fired."

The cause of the collapse was cinder blocks heaved onto the third level before cement poured on the C-joists as support had hardened. The cinder blocks were put there because the man in charge of the job, Eugene Ostreicher, had ordered them to be.

The day after the accident, Blaich was on the block when Ostreicher drove up.

"The fools!" Ostreicher said of the people working for the lowest money. "I told them not to put anything heavy on the floor. They're fools!"

Someone at the Building Department put in papers for violations and went home. His job was done, and he knew the paper would be in a file or on a computer forever because anything to do with Ostreicher, or any other Hasidic builder, was fixed by City Hall in advance.

Blaich, who admits to having had more faith, was at least surprised when the job, which had been closed for three days, suddenly
reopened with Ostreicher and his engineers, Hertzberg and Sanchez,
standing with one foot on the Mexican workers as usual. The Buildings Department sent no inspectors to see if they were making anything any safer. The Buildings Department issued a statement saying
that, under the law, they do not have to inspect such a building
until it is completed.

CHAPTER NINETEEN

His thirty-second birthday was on the twelfth of September, 1999, a Sunday, which is why Nelson Negrón is sure of most of the things that happened. The day before, Saturday, he had been out on the curb in front of the bodega on Bedford, and at eight o'clock a van pulled up and the guy called out for three people who wanted to work. Nelson and his friend Miguel got in the van, which took them to a factory in Long Island City where they spent the day moving sewing machines. To push a machine was a two-man job. Even so, by the middle of the afternoon their arms were made of lead. The guy gave Nelson and Miguel $60 and drove them back to the bodega. Nelson walked home. His roommate, Tony, had rice and beans ready. After that, Nelson watched television and fell asleep.

"My birthday," he said when he woke up at 7 A.M.

"Happy birthday," Tony said. "What are you going to do?"

"To work. I have no choice."

He got dressed and walked to the bodega, the DR, on Bedford Avenue. He had a pastrami sandwich and coffee and stood outside on Bedford, eating and hoping for the great job, a birthday present, a trailer truck from the south coming up and paying a hundred for the day to unload it. Instead, Leo Schwimmer pulled up in a green van and asked Negrón if he wanted to make $50. Put the $50 together with the $60 from the day before and I got $110 to begin the week, Nelson told himself. Beauty! If I ever put together five days, including the weekend, on top of this, then I got the best week I ever had working.

Negrón enthusiastically went over to the van, which he remembers had a sliding door. Leo knew from past jobs that Negrón could speak the language and was a good strong worker. Nelson had worked on beams, support beams, and taping for Leo. When Leo got to the Middleton Street site, a full crew was working. That it was Sunday meant nothing to Leo, and was not vital to the Mexicans, who believed that work is prayer. Leo told Nelson to get fifty-pound sacks of cement up to the third level of the new buildings. The building fronts were wide open. Framing would come later. They were working on a series of four-story brick houses that started at the corner bodega and ran up the street, taking in numbers 40–50 on Middleton Street. Across from the houses was a dreary brick grammar school.

Nelson got a sack on his shoulder and stepped up to the bottom level of the scaffold. That was one. Now he went up another level. Heaving and sweating already, up the scaffold he went, looking up at Eduardo's face and a roof held up by false hope.

"Too heavy!" Eduardo said. By this time, September 1999, he had gone from the curb at Bedford to construction sites all over Brooklyn, one job leading to another. Finally he was part of the crew on this group of buildings being built by Ostreicher. This was the job he had first heard about in Mexico.

"Nothing is too heavy for me," Negrón remembers saying. He weighs 220 and can handle weight.

He threw the sack onto the floor. The wood went up and down. Not a lot, but just enough to give him the idea that the floor where they were working was no good.

Negrón stayed on the scaffold and looked in. There were little cracks in the few beams he could see holding up this top floor. There were only three beams across.

Seeing that Negrón, too, had noticed the floor support, Eduardo asked, "Where's the rest of the beams?"

When Negrón complained, Eduardo's friend, Lucino, knew Negrón was saying the truth, but he didn't know what to do about it.

"We could get hurt," Negrón remembers Eduardo saying.

"You could get more than that," Negrón said.

He remembers that Alejandro then came over and said, "Could we get killed?"

"That's right," Negrón said.

"What are we supposed to do?" Alejandro said.

"I don't know," Negrón said.

"If we say it, the boss fires us," Alejandro said.

"This is how he wants it," Negrón said.

"It's wrong, but he told me to do it this way," Eduardo said.

"Around here," Negrón said, "around Bedford, the guy with the money runs your life."

Leo came back and told Nelson to take beams from a stack of shining aluminum and lug them to the top level. First, Negrón went to the corner bodega to get a bottle of water. They had learned that soft drinks don't do you much good.

Eduardo took Negrón's place with the cement sacks. Eduardo was sopping wet in the hot September afternoon as he made his way up the scaffolding with the fifty-pound sack on his shoulder. Eduardo struggled with the sack and was about to throw it on the third level when he slapped the wood with his hand. He felt it give.

"I could knock this thing down," Alejandro remembers Eduardo saying.

And he remembers saying to Eduardo, "You think so?"

"Sure."

Just inside on the third level, Eduardo had a circle of sand and a water hose and mixed the cement mushy, between dry and wet.

On the sidewalk, Leo looked around, made a phone call on his cell phone, and left.

Nelson Negrón threaded a rope through one of the utility holes in the beam and ran it up to a pulley fastened to the third level. He and a guy called Miguel then pulled the beam up. Miguel clambered up the scaffolding and got on the top level. Nelson came up behind him. Standing on the scaffolding, Nelson began to shove the beam onto the third level. He heard a sound, a screw dropping out of the scaffold. He went to put his right foot firm on the scaffolding, but there was nothing there. He was in the air, going over backward, and fell three stories to the dirt and debris.

He has no idea of how long he was there.

The first thing he saw was a man with no teeth bending over him and lifting him up by the arm. The man had on a long black sweater and good sneakers. Somebody said that the guy's name was Louis. Whoever he was, he had just appeared, and as soon as he got Negrón onto the sidewalk and propped against the base of the building, he went away.

At the same time, Negrón remembers that Leo showed up. When somebody said to call 911, Leo shouted, "No!" They had just finished three collapses around the corner and one on this block. He wanted no record of this one. He slid the door open while a couple of workers carried Nelson Negrón into the van.

When Leo delivered him in front of his apartment house, Nelson couldn't get out. He couldn't move one leg. His back was filled with barbed wire. Somebody from the sidewalk in front of his house had to come out and help him.

Negrón remembers Leo handing him $30.

"You didn't work the whole day."

He made a U-turn and drove off without looking at Nelson.

That was the last time for a while that Negrón saw anybody. Soon he had a cane and long empty days in his apartment.

CHAPTER TWENTY

That November of 1999, Eduardo's brother José admitted that he no longer could live away from his mother and father. He also missed a girl in San Matías named Teresa. "Besides," he told Eduardo, "I can help building the house." He sent all his savings, a thousand dollars, home to his father for the building. He went to Delgado Travel under the el and bought a ticket to Puebla. He spent most of his time packing his clothes. There were shirts and caps and jackets with insignias on them. The others in the room wouldn't have minded if he left some of them, but you cannot come back from America in such defeat that you don't even have a big thick Buffalo Sabres zipper jacket.

The little tricks of living with almost nothing were now brought into play. The day before he was to leave, José had to pick up his ticket. The woman in the agency said two identifications were required to get on the plane, and also to get back into Mexico. The Mexicans were copying the United States by having gatekeepers. The woman told José that his birth certificate alone was not enough;

he could be sent back from Mexico and arrested upon his arrival in New York. In a Russian gift shop across the street a man in the back took his picture and for $10 quickly made a plastic identification card that said, "Bearer has top security clearance for this company." A handwritten signature was at the bottom. The back of the card contained a brief lecture on the bearer's importance to the company.

His plane was at 4:30 on Saturday afternoon. Two and a half hours early, José and Eduardo carried one huge duffel bag to the travel agency; in his free hand Eduardo struggled with a much smaller but still heavy duffel bag. They threw it into the trunk of the Odessa Car Service livery car that he had ordered. Now on the sidewalk, a tiny woman with an old Indian face peered over the top of an immense box covered with black cloth. She had two young men helping her push it. The Mexicans call it a *muchila,* a knapsack, which she said held a stereo for her family in Cholula, but it was big enough to hold a bandstand. The woman's wrinkled hand held out a clump of bills. The woman wanted José to include her *muchila* as part of his baggage. She put $60 in his hand. She swore that the overweight charge would be thirty dollars, and the rest was his. He took the money, and the woman and the two with her pushed the box to the curb. They pointed to the trunk. The Russian cab driver stared at the cigarette in his hand. They pushed and tugged the black box into the back of the cab. Eduardo and José barely fit in.

At the airport, the line for the Mexican flight was about a block and a half long. Eduardo stayed with the luggage while José went for soda. Then Eduardo wandered over to the waiting room windows that looked out at the great plane with the AeroMexico markings that sat in hope and splendor in the sun. He told his brother that he could see his mother standing in the doorway of the courtyard as he walked toward her, with the dogs jumping onto him in joy. He wanted to get on this plane right now. So what if he couldn't do it? He'd go to the travel agent and get the next one.

The woman at the AeroMexico counter grimaced as she and another agent pulled José's two bags off the scale and threw them onto the conveyor. She told Jose that the overweight charge was $68. He had to put $8 of his own to the overweight bill. José muttered. He would still have to pay several dollars more or nobody at the Puebla airport would help with his luggage.

CHAPTER TWENTY-ONE

He woke up slowly. Instead of coming off the floor with a rush to get into the bathroom, Eduardo propped his chin on his fist and watched a pair of feet go by. He was thinking of something, because he didn't move, and another pair of feet whisked by. Ten minutes for each miss. When he heard the door opening, he pulled himself up and started for the bathroom, but someone else went right by him. He waited for the ten minutes and decided to add his banging to the day's confusion. Alejandro came out. "The last," he said to Eduardo. "Your timing is off."

They walked to the el on Brighton Beach Avenue.

Two short blocks over, on Fifth Street, Angel Tlapaltotoli came out of the dungeon of a rear basement apartment in the frame house where he lived with his wife and child. He walked up the alley to the street and turned for the el, which was only a few doors down. Lucino Hernández Robles was up at six o'clock in his room two flights up over Kings Highway and the subway. His cousin, Julisa, was busy with her baby. They said good morning to each other, and Lucino was gone to his job. Blocks away, in an unfurnished first-floor apartment, a block off the el, Juan Sánchez and his brother, Angel, each 5 feet 3 inches, threw on their clothes and left for the job. Juan had been here for seven years, and his younger brother only a few months. All the family was in New York working. The last to arrive, the father, was asleep in a back room. He worked in a restaurant. Juan was often anxious about the entire family barely making it; an uncle who earned $500 a week in a fish market was the greatest wage earner. Still, he knew it was better than the small farm in Mexico where he worked "morning to the sun, even to midnight" and for virtually no money. There also was a brother-in-law far over on Dean Street who was in the subway going to work at this hour.

The ones leaving the house in Brighton Beach rode the train to Smith/Ninth Street. They sat together and as usual had *huaza* talk about the young women on the train. They changed and took the local to Flushing Avenue and came down the stairs onto Middleton Street. In the morning dust ahead was the Job and the bodega next to the last building, 50 Middleton Street.

Eduardo had a container of coffee and one piece of toast in Lupita Bodega. He sat with four others at a small table covered with linoleum and wedged between shelves of jalapeño peppers, sugar, onions, Mr. Clean, Tampax, Pampers, Ziploc bags, and racks of pornographic books. It was a chill day and they wore heavy clothes. Summer people in winter clothes.

Hurshed, one of the Russians, had a can of soda that he held out for Eduardo. The others said Hurshed was taking the place of Eduardo's father.

The large red Speedy Pumping Concrete truck pulled up outside on Middleton Street. Its barrel revolved as the insides of rocks and cement were being mixed. There was a hose running from the truck up the front of the building to the third floor, where a heavy metal stand held up a spout for throwing off concrete. Eduardo held the handle of a machine that looked like a large electric floor waxer.

Somebody called up, and with a roar the concrete truck's engine became loud and the cement came pouring from the spout. Eduardo, on the third floor, pushed with his big spreader; the others working had wood trowels. The noise filled all ears.

Over in a corner in the rear of the floor there were these fingers of light coming through cracks where the right wall of the structure should have been fastened to the rest of the place, including the roof.

Juan Sánchez looked up and was surprised to see the light coming through cracks. He became frightened when he saw the bars of light growing larger. Already, after working four months on this building, he noticed that rainwater was in the bottom part of the building but not up on the third level. He didn't know what that meant. He knew he didn't like that the building shook when they poured concrete.

He says that this time he called out, "No bueno." But the noise from the concrete pump on the third level and the spreading machine Eduardo was pushing were too loud.

There was no swaying or quivering. No time even for a warning gasp from somebody. One second to the other, Alejandro says. An instant, a shrug of concrete and metal, and the floor under Eduardo went.

Down Eduardo went, so quickly that he made no sound.

Down went Alejandro and Lucino and Gustavo and two Angels and Juan.

Down they went so quickly that nobody screamed.

The third floor fell into the second floor and the second fell into the first and everything fell into the basement. The rear wall blew out, as did a wall that was supposed to be tied to the building. There was a cascade of cinder blocks and metal.

What were supposed to be metal beams holding up the floors were as strong as aluminum foil.

Eduardo fell face first into three feet of concrete on the basement floor and drowned.

There were shrieks in the basement from the dozen who were injured and in the concrete.

Above, the cement pump still stood on one part of the floor that had not snapped. The pump kept pouring concrete down, the thickest of gray rains. The workers were stuck in it. As it covered the chests of the workers, it started to flatten them and stifle their breathing. If one exhaled, the weight of the concrete on his chest prevented him from inhaling again.

Angel Sánchez fell into concrete, and his brother landed on top of him. Angel was partially buried, and the concrete came down in a gray storm. His brother-in-law pulled him up.

Alejandro went under the concrete and would have been gone forever except Angel Tlapaltotoli caught sight of him. He is small, this Angel is, and he was hurt and stunned from the fall, but he saw the spot where Alejandro disappeared, and somehow he took one leap out of the concrete and landed in next to Alejandro and stabbed both arms down through it and onto Alejandro. He yanked Alejandro's head up and was rubbing the concrete from his mouth and nostrils. Alejandro was unconscious. But he was alive in Angel's hands.

How many did Gustavo Ramirez grab?

All anybody remembers is the cries for help and Gustavo grabbing at people. Grabbing for Lucino, who was in shock and unable to move. Or at Hurshed, the big guy, whose head was above the concrete, but when he became catatonic, his head had to be held up.

The woman in the bodega called 911.

When Chief Dillon from the Fire Department arrived, he saw the concrete truck on the street oblivious to what was happening. It was still pumping concrete upstairs. Dillon's aide, Chris Steidinger, ran up to the truck and shouted at the driver to stop it.

Now Bill Pieszak of Emergency Services, just off the truck, came through an opening into the basement. Another cop, Dave Kayen, went through the first floor window.

Sticking out of the concrete were arms and legs and the white oval of a mouth. It was strange, Pieszak remembers, but the wet concrete saved a couple of them because they landed on something soft. At the same time, Pieszak and Kayen were in wet concrete up to their thighs and could barely move. They began to try to remove people by first bending forward with their arms stretched out and digging at the wet concrete with their hands.

Dig it and shove it to make a clearing around the body. As they made this clearing, the concrete came back like a heartless tide. They kept pushing the concrete. Pieszak lifted a body. Lifted it four inches. He took a breath, reached into the concrete again, and tried for another four inches.

The concrete parted under Kayen's hands and he saw a prize, a belt with a big buckle. The buckle was covered with concrete, but it had a value greater than any medallion ever struck for royalty. This was a buckle you could grab and pull up, and he raised the body of a mauled human out of the sucking concrete just enough to let him live. With Pieszak tugging at the shoulders and Kayen at the belt, they lifted.

Four inches. Maybe a little more. Lift again. Four inches. Now again. Four inches. Lifting, lifting, lifting. Now slide a board under the body and up comes a mummy able to breathe. Because of the concrete, the worker weighed twice his normal weight.

Now there were firemen and cops everywhere, tugging, heaving, and these voices were calling out, "Angel?" "Juan!" One Mexican, battered, dazed, and bleeding, tried to slip away after they pulled him out. Firefighters grabbed him. They were afraid he was hurt and would collapse trying to walk home. The guy kept trying to get away. He was more afraid of an immigration agent than of an injury.

Eduardo's body was pulled out of the cellar by ropes. He was one hundred pounds heavier with the cement on him. The body was taken to the morgue at Bellevue Hospital.

In Woodhull Hospital, Lucino was in bed in a haze and with his body hurting. José J. Eduardo, the husband of Lucino's cousin Julisa, was allowed in. She had medical knowledge and the husband had none, so of course she remained with the children and he saw

Lucino in intensive care. José told him in amazement, "Do you know, somebody died." He told Lucino it was Eduardo. It would be many months before Lucino could say the name without crying. Miguel called Eduardo's father, Daniel, and said that something had happened. The father went into denial and hung up on him. Then Gustavo's sister, Teresa Hernández, who had gotten several calls about the accident, called the father from her basement room in Queens Village. She said that Eduardo had died. The father in San Matías shouted, "No!" and hung up. The father called Brighton Beach and got only Mariano Ramirez, a brother of Gustavo and Teresa who'd slept on the floor with Eduardo and who had two brothers hurt in the collapse. Mariano didn't want to be the one to tell Eduardo's father. He told Daniel that he would find out and call back. Finally, after many calls, Miguel, the husband of Martha, Mariano's sister, called Daniel and told him. This time, Daniel believed the bad news. He closed the cell phone and turned around and told his wife that the first child born to her was dead.

Silvia was surprised that her mother was calling her this late, after she had returned home from the night job at the Olive Garden. It was her mother who called rather than anybody from Brighton Beach, because Eduardo never had informed anybody that she was his girlfriend.

The mother said she did not know how Eduardo died. Silvia remembered him saying he had to climb up the building. In her mind she saw him dead on the ground, sprawled dramatically. Nobody told her mother or her how he actually died. Her mother asked if she was coming for the funeral, and Silvia said of course she would be there. She hung up and sat through part of the night thinking about it. That they had not seen each other in months was suddenly not important. They could get past that and live their lives. But the death left her blank. She had never experienced anything that had a finality to it. This did. At her age, all the days and months were part of looking ahead.

BACK IN NEW YORK, a social worker, Awilda Cordero, drove Angel and Mariano to the morgue. They went into a conference room, and one of the assistants came in with color pictures of Eduardo's corpse. The two looked at the picture, said, "*Sí*," and the identification was through. It took several more days for the body to be released because immigration people had to be notified that the young man was here without papers. This is poor form for a dead body.

That Sunday afternoon, with the sky gray and the wide commercial street outside desolate, Eduardo's body was in a white casket in a closet of grief at the Lopez Funeral Home in Brooklyn. He was in a good white shirt, and the black cap he loved sat atop the casket. Everybody who was not in the hospital came there in rough clothes and sat in silence. Gustavo was angry and kept mopping his forehead, which was still bleeding.

The cost of getting the body to Mexico was paid by the Red Cross and the New York City Central Labor Trades Council, whose members in the construction trades are mostly white and from New Jersey, and whose officers are in their element at cocktail parties in Manhattan with politicians. The labor leaders paused to pay for the funeral and get in the newspapers.

The case was in the jurisdiction of the Kings County District Attorney's office, whose normal tenacity in pursuit of justice slowed to a stroll when faced with the history of the Board of Elections, in whose records are carried no list of winners who attack Hasidim.

At this moment, into the ominous gloom and wet smell of the collapsed building on Middleton Street came James Vanderberg of the Department of Labor. He was another of these people who exude mildness and can destroy you. He was slim and young. His job was to find out how this poor Mexican got killed. But he had to do it with a lightened step. Under the OSHA rules, a violation of safety rules causing the death of a worker is a misdemeanor. The maximum for the misdemeanor is six months in prison. There is no restitution for the victim. But if a felony could be made out of

Ostreicher's lying to the federal agent, Caterina, then there was a chance that something could be gained out of the sourness and misery of the matter. For the felony would be punishable by from zero to six years in prison. Restitution for the Gutiérrez death could somehow be made a part of any plea agreement, and there certainly would be one; Ostreicher could face no jury. The fine could then be substantial and Eduardo's family, which had only been hurt until now, could receive some financial help. Eduardo had drowned in concrete during great arguing on Mount Olympus about world commerce and work. Eduardo had no understanding of the names of the technologies that caused fists to wave on the streets of Seattle and Genoa. Nor could he name the diversities of trade, nor the new merchandise that comes off the shelf not by hand but by a tapping key whose message flies to the sky and back to the shelf. Yet Eduardo represented the most invaluable part of the economy of the world. He was cheap labor.

IN A VACANT CORNER OF THE airport in Mexico City, international trade was represented by the casket of Eduardo, who had died in Williamsburg, in Brooklyn, and was in Mexico to be buried. He was put on a van. Mariano, who had brought the body home, cried as he got into the van, which drove down to Eduardo's house and the funeral.

In College Station, Silvia sat one last night before deciding that she couldn't go to the funeral. Getting to San Matías was simple. But then she would have to sneak across the border again, and that could take days and weeks, particularly if she got turned back. Surely she would lose both her jobs. She thought of the railroad tracks in the night with snakes in the brush. That settled it. She would sob for Eduardo and then live for the living.

The order of grieving in San Matías calls for nine days of prayers before the burial. By the time the body arrived in the yard at Calle Libre, eight days had passed, and the father agreed with the priest that the young man should be buried on the next morning.

The night before the funeral, Eduardo's casket was in a room that had been cleared out and was across from his new blue room. There was no upstairs because there was no money to build. Eduardo's new room shrugs off storms and sun. It is painted blue with white trim. It is a glorious room. The casket was surrounded by candles, and there was wailing and fainting.

Instead of many prayers and drinks, there were only prayers that night. On the morning of the funeral one of his cousins, a woman with a face of the Aztecs, bit her lip and began hauling a bucket of water out of the well. One hand over the other, arms straining as she pulled the rope. Now the large pail came out with the water sparkling in the sun, and some of this reflected onto the wall of the room Eduardo died for.

They carried Eduardo's body through the heat and among the children running with dogs alongside, the large crowd pushing to get closer to the casket of Eduardo Daniel Gutiérrez, who drowned in concrete in Brooklyn at age twenty-one while trying to make money.

They went to the old yellow church with red trim, with candlelight flickering on the gold wreaths and babies crying and the sound of children's feet. The people stood outside the doors and threw rice to symbolize the marriage Eduardo never had.

Then they walked the streets to the cemetery. They were in the middle of the cobblestone walk that went up to the cemetery gates. The walk went past stacked tires and the clotheslines of families living in shacks, and the crowd threw white carnations at the casket.

Nine young women stepped out of the crowd. One, whose name was Sol, wore a white sweater and a heartbreakingly young face. She went up to the casket and took the place of a young man. She held the casket handles underhand. Eight other young women took the places of the young men who had been carrying it.

Now there were nine young women, each of whom held the handles underhand.

A mariachi band at the end of the procession played a song called "Las Flores." As the trumpets sounded in the hot sunlight, the band leader, wearing a powder blue suit and black gloves, began singing the song.

On the left side of the casket, Sol swayed back on her right foot. So did the other young women on her side. The young women on the other side swayed forward with the casket.

Now the young women on the left side stopped going back and swayed forward. All hands gripped the casket handles, and the young faces were determined as they swayed with the heavy box. The young women on the right side stepped back.

As the left side came forward, all the young women caused the casket to dance a couple of feet closer to the cemetery gate.

Young women learn this dance just by living here. It is done only with the caskets of women who die unmarried or a young man like Eduardo Daniel Gutiérrez, who drowned in concrete at age twenty-one in Williamsburg in Brooklyn.

The young women carrying his casket were friends of Eduardo. Their faces were determined. Soon, however, they cried as they made Eduardo's casket dance. Sway forward on the left leg, sway back on the right foot, sway forward, sway back, sway, sway, sway, dance the young man to his grave.

In front of the cemetery, as the mariachi singer cried out the last notes of his song about flowers, the young women had their places at the casket taken by older men. The older men now rocked the casket as if it were a rowboat.

Three young men sat atop the cemetery arch and threw candy down. The kids raced for it.

Inside the graveyard there was a tangle of small graves covered with dead flowers. The grave had been dug by friends of the father, Eduardo Daniel. The cemetery is staffed only by flies.

Before the casket was lowered, Eduardo's mother, Teresa, was at the foot of the casket, and her face, uncovered, held a thousand years of grief. All through her roots, lifetime after lifetime, somebody young had died in every one of the families that came before her. At moments like this, her only emotion was dull acceptance.

Mariano Ramirez Torres tried to bury his round young face into the top of the casket. In the throng pushing forward to be near the grave was his mother, Angelina. With the two sons hurt in Brooklyn and not working, and the other son here to mourn, she said that there were no money orders from Brooklyn. She is raising the four children of one of the injured sons, Gustavo.

At the graveside the grandmother, Angelina, was racked with grief and necessity.

There were at least half a dozen men standing in the fresh dirt at the lip of the grave. Two men in white polo shirts were in the hole. When they pushed and tugged the casket into place, they got on either side of the casket and began slapping new red bricks, baked in this shack town, atop the casket. They wanted a brick wall to protect the top of the casket when the dirt and sand would be thrown down on it.

Eduardo Gutiérrez had already drowned once.

On June 15, 2001, the New York City Central Labor Trades Council ran a media bus tour of South Eighth Street in Williamsburg, where another Mexican immigrant from Puebla, Rogelio Daze Villaneuva, was crushed to death. He lost his life only blocks away from where Eduardo had perished.

A Hi-Lo forklift caused a ramp to collapse on the demolition job of an old hot dog factory that was uninspected.

In the doorway of a building next door, a gray-haired man wearing a shirt with the words *Kabila's Knishes* on the front pocket said, "No papers."

"The contractor?"

"No, the Mexicans. They have no papers, no green card. No paper, no pay. Cheap pay. Five, six dollar an hour. Nobody looks at the building."

Rogelio, an immigrant with no papers of any sort, had been making about a third of union wages. He had four children.

The union announced that the bus ride was to "shine a bright, public light on violations of basic human rights of workers in New York City."

Eduardo's father, Daniel, arrived in Brooklyn unnoticed at that time. He was here for depositions for lawsuits. The lawyer had sent tickets. He got off the plane with two hundred dollars. Two hundred American, he said to himself. I can stay here for a month.

He was on Lorimer Street, the one behind the ruined buildings on Middleton Street where his son died. This is not using the name Lorimer Street as geography in a story. Rather, the attempt at justice was made on that dull, treeless block.

Daniel crouched and pushed through a narrow, ragged opening in a chain-link fence and trudged through this lot filled with debris that was covered with weeds. He came to the rear of the collapsed buildings where Eduardo drowned in concrete.

The father was forty-six. Suddenly, he seemed so much older. Pain spilled from the dark eyes and ran through the small creases around his eyes and into the ravines and rivulets of his cheeks and mouth. He looked over seventy.

Then the sunlight splashed the brown face and the lines softened and he was forty-six again. A sadness weighs on his eyes, and he looks down to hide this.

The construction site is silent. A metal sign says it is in the hands of a demolition company. On the left, the last two units have wood ladders of four steps leading up to the second level. The one next to last has a basement yawning dark and wet. Daniel looks into the open first floor. He shakes his head, then holds his thumb and forefinger far apart. He points at a space between the wall and the floor above.

At the ruins of the last site, the one that was going to be numbered 50 Middleton, he went up the ladder. For so many nights and days in San Matías he tried to imagine this place. But now there was only a pile of cinder blocks and bricks and twisted metal that has an evil shine.

The sound of a bus idling comes from Middleton Street.

Suddenly, and in a quiet voice, Daniel says that he can see Eduardo at work. "He is talking to the other workers," Daniel says. "He is happy and young."

Now he steps up to the vision that has dissolved. He sees the pile of bricks at the place where the floors caved and his son dropped face first into a lake of concrete covering the basement.

The father's face does not change. He does not talk. The moment causes tongue and face to be frozen. This is where his first-born son died. Walk up to the place and look at it. Then call the boy's mother in Mexico and tell her what it looked like. What else is there to do? It is your life as a Mexican.

Now tears finally run from the corners of his eyes.

He stays only for a few minutes. Leaving the street, they drive him up a few blocks to Woodhull Hospital, which sits under the el.

"This is where they took Eduardo," somebody told Daniel.

Immediately he twisted to see the building. He took a pencil out of his pocket and tried to write the name down on a scrap of paper. The driver, Awilda Cordero, stopped the car and printed it in large letters.

"Woodhull," he said, reading it.

He put the piece of paper into his breast pocket. "For the mother," he said. The hospital made him cry.

He had six days left in Brooklyn before flying back to San Matías. He was staying in a blue frame house on a small crooked street in Brighton Beach with Mariano and three others from San Matías, who had moved a few blocks from the one room where everybody slept on the floor.

At 11 A.M. on a Thursday, he was watching an animal show on the Discovery Channel. He was fascinated by a large python at work. The el train ran almost directly over the house, and the noise kept filling the room.

He had no way of knowing that suddenly on this day a year

and a half of frustration was coming to an end a few miles away, in downtown Brooklyn, where the clerk in the fourth floor federal courtroom of Judge Leo Glasser called out, "United States of America versus Ostreicher, Criminal Information 01CR717."

Eugene Ostreicher, blocky and decisive of step, walked up to the bench. He had on a black yarmulke and a black suit with a white shirt open at the collar. His beard was two large white puffs coming from his cheeks. He had sharp dark eyebrows over pale blue eyes. He stood motionless.

"Frank Mandel for Eugene Ostreicher," his lawyer, a thin man, said.

"Assistant United States Attorney Richard Faughnan for the government."

Ostreicher was sworn in. He was here to plead guilty to a criminal information. This is different from a grand jury indictment, which causes a full jury trial. A criminal information gives a defendant the chance to slither out of deepest trouble with a plea.

The judge said, "Do you realize that you must tell the truth, that it is a crime to tell a lie after you swear to tell the truth?"

"Yes," Ostreicher said.

Glasser then asked him if he was under any medication that would interfere with his ability to understand what he was doing. Then he asked him to read a copy of the charge against him. The judge then said that rather than plead guilty right here he could stand on his constitutional right to a grand jury. He told Ostreicher that a grand jury is made of between sixteen and twenty-three people, and if at least twelve say there is a probable cause that a crime has been committed, there will be an indictment. Did Ostreicher understand?

He understood too well. For eighteen months he had been twisting and ducking the chances of such a thing, for he understood that the indictment inevitably leads to a trial and the chances for imprisonment would be high.

Now Glasser read the charge. "On March 14, 1996, in the Eastern

District of New York you knowingly made a false statement to an OSHA officer by stating that at buildings number 25–49 Lorimer Street there had been no collapse."

Glasser pressed Ostreicher. "You have a right to say not guilty. In that case there will be a public jury trial."

Ostreicher showed no anxiety.

"I do not accept a guilty plea from an innocent man," Glasser said.

(The last time I saw Glasser, he took a guilty plea from Sammy Gravano, not quite an innocent.)

"How do you plead?" Ostreicher was asked.

"Guilty."

After a year and a half of investigations by one agency after another, Ostreicher convicted himself of spitting on the sidewalk.

Right to the end, most thought that the plea agreement was supposed to be for an OSHA civil case only, and therefore there would be no prison time. However, the Labor Department agent, James Vanderberg, had never quit pressing for a felony criminal charge and won out in the back rooms of justice. The civil charge was replaced by a criminal felony charge. It included what Vanderberg wanted: a fine of a million dollars so at least the victims could get something. Usually there is nothing for them.

In court, the judge gave him one part of the sentence. He would never be allowed to build again, which was something the Fire Department's Blaich had called for at least three years ago. Then a million-dollar fine was to be paid to the victims of Middleton Street. He was not charged with the deadly collapse, but he was fined for it because on a plea, you can put in almost anything— write down "Rome burning." There was no way anybody was going to let Ostreicher walk away from Eduardo Daniel Gutiérrez's death with no penalty at all. Glasser said the additional sentencing date would be in October. Ostreicher faced anything from zero to five years, the judge said. The chances were that there would be no prison time. That was to happen.

When the guilty plea was over, Mandel stood in the aisle and said to somebody, "Where did you get the police badge from?"

"From the guys he showed it to."

"Who showed it?"

"Richie the Rabbi."

"Who? There is no such person." Mandel playfully punched one of the people with him. "He says there is a Richie the Rabbi in the family."

Mandel laughed and the guy laughed. Ostreicher shrugged. He was not going to say anything to anybody, because that was what had gotten him in trouble. Of course there is a Richie the Rabbi, proper name Chaim. Only this time there was no federal guy asking an official question.

Richie the Rabbi went to Belgium after the collapse. One day he called Captain Bill Gorta at police headquarters in Manhattan and said, Gorta remembers, "I just had a baby. I have to go to City Hall in Brussels to register him. Do you think you could call them and ask them as a courtesy to the NYPD to let me go right through without having to wait on line?"

Later in the day, Daniel stood on the street outside the house in Brighton Beach. The two hundred American had lasted only a couple of days. Mariano, from the house, had found a temporary job for him, installing floors in a supermarket around the corner. Daniel worked ten hours for $50. He hated it. He realized this was how his son had started here. He wasn't going back to the job. He would sit here until he had to get his plane.

"A million," he was told. "For all the victims."

"All the victims."

"Yes, but your son died so that should be the largest amount."

That was a wrong estimate. The Russian, Hurshed, would have to live with his permanent damages and would need every dollar. He would get the most, $800,000. As Eduardo was gone, his father would receive $100,000.

But now, not knowing this, he shrugged. "I only stayed here to see where the accident was. If they give me something, fine. But I'm going back on Thursday. I don't like it here."

He held up four fingers. "I have four more."

"José is the oldest?" he was asked.

"He is married. I just have my first grandson."

"Who carries the bricks in the yard now?"

"I do. With Miguel. You saw him when he was young. He is grown up."

"Then who are the little ones at the end of the line?"

"The girls. Maria Cruz. Zenaida."

He looked down at the sidewalk. Then he took out a pack of Marlboros. When he lit one, it was the end of his conversation. He had lost too much around here, in Brooklyn, in America, and he wanted to get home.

INDEX

ABOUT THE AUTHOR

JIMMY BRESLIN has been writing a syndicated newspaper column for more than forty years. He is at *Newsday* and is the author of *The Gang That Couldn't Shoot Straight* and, most recently, the novel *I Don't Want to Go to Jail*. He lives in New York City.